IN MEMORY OF:
MY FATHER, JOHN KNOWLES SNR. WHO SURVIVED
WWII AND THE GERMAN STALAGS.

DEDICATED TO:
RUTH, WITHOUT WHOSE LOVE, SUPPORT AND
COMPUTING SKILLS THIS BOOK WOULD
NEVER HAVE HAPPENED.

THE LOST BOYS OF LOSTOCK

THOSE WHO DIED IN THE GREAT WAR 1914 – 1918

by
John A. Knowles

Copyright © 2014 John A. Knowles
The right of John Knowles to be identified as the author of this work has been asserted by him in accordance with the Copyright, Designs and Patents Act, 1988.

No part of this book may be reproduced or transmitted in any form or by any means, electronic or mechanical, including photocopying, recording or any information storage or retrieval system, without prior permission in writing from the author John A. Knowles, 77 Birches Lane, Lostock Green, CW9 7SN.

ISBN
978-0-949001-51-1

C.C.PUBLISHING, MARTINS LANE,
HARGRAVE, CHESTER, CH3 7RX
TEL: 01829 741651. EMAIL: editor@cc-publishing.co.uk
WEBSITE: http://www.cc-publishing.co.uk

Contents

Acknowledgements	(iv)
Prologue	(v)
Ode to a Geordie Soldier in The Great War	(vii)
Lostock Gralam in 1914	9
The Old Contemptible Deakins	12
The Connollys of Brook Street	18
The Terraced Rows	26
The Terriers	50
The Pickerings of Manchester Road	53
The Southern Boys	59
The Foxleys of Station Road	66
The 'Canadians' Come Home	74
Lostock's Subalterns	80
The Back-to-Back Terraces by St. John's	85
By the Side of the Church	90
On Station Road	98
In Stanley Grove	104
On Manchester Road	108
A Truly 'Well Known' Lostockian	118
The Lost of Lostock Green	124
The First of the Many … and the Last	130
They Also Served	134
The Letters of Sam Hitchen	138
Killed in Action by Regiment	142
Killed in Action by Street	143
Where They Lie	144
Men Who Were First Sons	145
Moving On	146

The Lost Boys of Lostock

Acknowledgements

Caroline Mannion and the Staff of Cheshire Military Museum

Mat Carmody

Karen Dean

Staff at Northwich Library

Staff at Cheshire Records Office

Staff at the National Archives, Kew

Laura Pooley and the Staff of Cheshire West Museums

Northwich Guardian

Aidan Knowles-Levitt – his poem

John Jefferson – advice on illnesses of the Great War

Richard Le Corney – the proof reader

Wayne Porter, Castle Tiles, Northwich

Staff at the Imperial War Museum

David Stanley – Lostock photos 2014

(All profits to the Commonwealth War Graves Commission)

The Lost Boys of Lostock

Prologue

LONGWORTH'S hairdressing salon is tucked away down Station Road, on the corner of Arthur Street, opposite the churchyard of St. John the Evangelist, in the heart of old Lostock Gralam.

I had paid my monthly visit to the salon to have my seriously thinning locks tended by Gary and Neil and had leisurely crossed the small, private car park, enjoying the February sunshine. As I opened the car door, I glanced across at the Memorial Cross some twenty yards away in the churchyard as I had done so many times before. This time, however, the lychgate stood ajar allowing me an uninterrupted view of the area around the base of the Cross. To my surprise, I recognised the white, distinctive shape of a Commonwealth War Graves Commission (CWGC) headstone. On numerous visits to the battlefields of the Somme I had observed literally thousands of these memorial stones commemorating the lost generations of the 1914-1918 War, but to find one in a backwater such as this, instantly aroused my curiosity. Within minutes and over ninety years after his burial, I was studying the memorial to 19-year-old Thomas Henry Wrench. Immediately two questions presented themselves – firstly, what was Tommy doing here when so many of his contemporaries were buried overseas and, secondly, was he the only serving soldier buried in St. John's churchyard? It only took a quick glance round to identify two more headstones marking the graves of J. Garner and T. Hall, thus fuelling my curiosity even further. Why were they all here rather than in France or Mesopotamia?

As I left the cemetery, I checked the inscriptions on the Memorial Cross and, immediately, I was hooked. Whilst I had expected to see a list of names thereon, I certainly did not anticipate the sheer number of the lads from the parish who had made the supreme sacrifice during the Great War. I double-checked but, no mistake, there were 68 names, three of which I later discovered were from outside the parish, their names inscribed due to them having worshipped at St John's Church.

Once again I contemplated the grave of Tommy Wrench and could not help wondering if anyone still remembered his very existence? And what of the other 64 parishioners? Did they merely live on a stone cross? Were they lost to memory forever? They had walked to school along Station Road and School Lane, the very streets that I had strolled through that sunny morning. Many must have enjoyed a drink at the Slow and Easy, bowled on the Alkali green and trudged along the Manchester Road to the Brunner Mond chemical works. In the first dozen years of the twentieth century these young men had represented the future of Lostock Gralam – but those futures were to be truncated by the bloodiest carnage man had ever experienced.

The Lostock Gralam Memorial Cross.

I remember to this day standing before their memorials and feeling humbled. Could I do anything for those boys? Well, I could make a small contribution to ensure that 'their names liveth for ever more' by finding out whatever still remained about each one of them and committing it to print so that there would exist at least a simple publication to which future generations could refer.

What follows is my first ever attempt to record a piece of historical research linked by lyrical storytelling.

Note: The photographs in this book all merit inclusion, but they do not always lend themselves to quality reproduction. This is particularly noticeable with the individual images of the Lostock Fallen, taken from local newspaper photocopies, the only source available.

An Ode to a Geordie in The Great War
by Aidan Knowles-Levitt

I'm a gannin' off ta War
Hope it not gonna be a bore
Ma Vest is itchy and ma feet are sore . . .
BUUUUT I'm a gannin' off ta war.

I'm in the Trenches a-fightin' the war
I've gota admit, I'm a wee bit sore
And all me friends do snore
BUUUT I'm a-fightin' inna war.

I'm a-gannin' over the top
All me friends have had the lot
And anyway, it's only a small hop
Tilll get over the top!

I'm in hospital in the war
I am so incredibly bored
I cannit see or feel no more
I'm a-dyin' BUUUT at least we've won the war!

Lostock Gralam in 1914

THE year 1914 started optimistically in Lostock Gralam. Full employment was available, either in the great Brunner Mond Works, at Hesketh's Bone Mill or at the numerous farms that dotted the landscape.

Brunner Mond and Company were, indeed, the Lords of the Manor and principal landowners. They afforded employment to virtually one quarter of the village's 2,200 inhabitants, many of whom were even more indebted to the Company – for the very roofs over their heads, the allotments where they grew vegetables to augment the family budget, the Social Club and Bowling Greens at which they took their leisure and the riverside walks where they idled away precious Sundays.

As far as the local children were concerned, some important business from the Old Year had still to be completed. The annual Christmas Treat was traditionally held over until early January. Over 650 of the village children assembled in the Lostock Pavilion where they were given a sumptuous tea and entertained by the renowned Stockport magician, Mr. Oswald Gordon. For their parents, there was the Annual Parochial Gathering with over 300 of them enjoying an excellent tea provided by Mrs. Tudor-Evans, the vicar's wife, and her small army of 'cutters-up'. Afterwards, a show was presented by a Pierrot troop from Manchester and the evening ended with dancing to Mr. Wilson's band, with the Station Road butcher, Mr. Harry Wright, acting as Master of Ceremonies.

Elsewhere, the year had started superbly for the three local football teams. Lostock Gralam were top of Cheshire League Division 1; Northwich Victoria were leading Division 1 of the Lancashire Combination; and Witton Albion were in similar predominance in Division 2. All three teams were to retain their positions to the end of the season that would herald the beginning of the Great War. At the local cinema, crowds were flocking to watch the wonderful film, 'Sixty Years a Queen', even though the subject had departed this life some twelve years previously. So enthusiastic was its reception that the film was shown twice nightly, with one matinee on Wednesdays and two on Saturdays. Even then queues still formed in the streets before each showing.

The Lost Boys of Lostock

Those of a romantic persuasion could be tempted by letters in the local press from ex-Lostock men who had emigrated to Canada some two years before and were now 'spreading the word' about the wonderful opportunities there. Colliery work was available in Nova Scotia with up to nine shillings a day paid to hard workers and as much as twelve shillings for experienced miners. Lodgings were readily obtainable for single men at fourteen shillings a week, whilst for families there was a choice of three bedroomed houses, all 'with running water attached' for twenty eight shillings monthly. Added to which there were no labour disputes. For those who preferred the outdoor life the Canadian Government's Representative in Liverpool was talking to local gatherings about the record harvests being enjoyed in Canada at large and the consequential need for labourers. To add to the temptation there was plenty of domestic work available for the women. Possibly the most positive inducement came in a letter from an old son of Lostock, Tom Smallwood, who revealed that in Saskatchewan anybody who worked in the province for four years qualified for a piece of land of some 160 acres. Some of the young men had already packed and departed but, later in the year, when news reached the North American continent of the outbreak of war in Europe, the call was equally irresistible.

The winter and spring of 1914 were notable for their very ordinariness. Arguably the busiest men in the village were Constables Roberts and Brookes, who paraded a never-

Four Lane Ends, Lostock Gralam... 'Prosecution Corner'.

Early days... soldiers of the Cheshire Regiment.

ending line of drunks, motorists and dog licence dodgers before the Northwich magistrates. P.C. Roberts appears to have been particularly quick to prosecute but was often unsupported by the judiciary. The judges dismissed his case against three fourteen-year-old boys for playing football 'on a Sunday' in the passage behind their homes and also refused his speeding prosecutions of five motorists in a two week period. Nobody liked P.C. Roberts's habit of hiding in the bushes at the Station Road / Manchester Road junction, Four Lane Ends, which, as a result, became known locally as 'Prosecution Corner'. There was laughter in court when, in March 1914, Roberts reported the dog of Sam Broady, the coal merchant, which he claimed had been loose at midnight and had caused him to lose part of his trousers as he leapt over the coal yard wall to escape from the protesting hound! Again, case dismissed!

As winter turned into spring the young men revelled in the opening of the Bowling Greens at the 'Slow and Easy', the Works Club, and at the Northwich Gladstone Club. More than thirty of those participants were to enjoy their last ever summer there as the dark clouds gathered over Europe. By the autumn of 1914 the greens were all closed, the bowls packed away and the players, now khaki-clad and fired by the declaration of 4th August 1914, had left for the War.

The Old Contemptible Deakins

THE financial incentives of the local chemical industry had brought Samuel and Lizzie Deakin and their four children from Runcorn to Northwich in 1883. They had rented a two-up-and-two-down in Gladstone Street but, with their ever-increasing family, they were to move to the relative luxury of 46 Huxley Street, with its three bedrooms, by 1895.

The family finally moved into Ann Street, in the parish of Lostock Gralam, early in 1905. By now the four children, who had moved from Runcorn, had all left home; three girls to work in domestic service about Northwich, while William had become a regular soldier in the 1st battalion of the Cheshire Regiment as one of the Hartford (Northwich) volunteers who served with honour in the Boer War. There were still six children in the house. The move across Cheshire had produced another three of each for Sam and Lizzie but, although life was by no means easy, the family lived comfortably on the

The 1st Cheshires heading for York Docks, Belfast.

edge of, but within walking distance of their old friends, in the market town of Northwich.

William had completed his service in South Africa with the Cheshires, but would remain as a National Reservist for a considerable period. Work was readily available as a shiftman at Brunner's Works in Winnington and his childhood sweetheart, Emily, became his wife in 1907. They managed to rent a small house in Waterloo Road in the Northwich Castle district and, quite quickly, they had three extra mouths to feed. However, with nine aunts and uncles as frequent visitors and an especially caring Granddad Sam, who always called on Sunday to take their dad, William, for a lunchtime drink the young family prospered. Visits to Ann Street were frequent and Grandma Lizzie's Sunday teas were much anticipated, especially as they were preceded by walks down to Wincham Flashes to watch the fishing.

As for the rest of Europe, the peace was shattered by the assassination of the Archduke Ferdinand in Sarajevo in 1914. William was immediately recalled to his regiment, which he joined in Londonderry on August 8th 1914. A brief re-equipping period followed and within days he sailed from York Docks in Belfast on the S.S. Massillia. He was not the only Deakin on that boat. Samuel, too, had served a short period as a regular in the Cheshires and had made such good progress that he had reached the rank of corporal before he had left the army in early 1914, married and taken employment as a

Mons 'High Street' in 1913.

cleaner at Northwich Steam Railway Sheds. As a reservist, Samuel had also been recalled immediately at the Outbreak and had trodden the same gangplank as William boarding the S.S.Massillia. But the family involvement with the boat did not stop even there. Younger brother, Harry, too, was a Cheshire's regular, a signaller, and had spent some time on garrison duty in Londonderry in anticipation of the possible Civil War in Ulster when the news of the mobilization came. The sense of shock within the extended Deakin family was palpable. Three of the boys were in France by August 15th and John, the remaining brother, was considering his options.

Pte. William Deakin (left) and Crp. Sam Deakin.

News from the Front was not long in coming. The first great battle of the war had taken place at a town called Mons, where the 1st Cheshires had suffered appalling casualties; 25 officers and 950 men had been present on the morning of August 24th; only 7 of the former and 200 of the latter remained when the evening roll call was taken. Amongst the missing was Harry Deakin.

The Cheshires were ordered to retreat from Mons but, within days, the push north began and, by September 15th, they crossed the River Aisne heading towards La Bassée. On October 21st the Battalion was involved in a fierce fire-fight near the village of Violaines. In the face of vastly superior numbers of the enemy, over 230 officers and men were lost. All of the officers and the great majority of the Cheshires who had landed at Le Havre on 16th August were gone.

On 1st November Sam and Lizzie were comforting Samuel's wife, who had received a telegram informing her that her husband was missing at the Front. The parents' suffering was doubled: both Harry and Samuel missing and only scant news from William.

Christmas 1914 brought no joy to the Deakins. What family celebrations they held were muted. Grandad Sam was quietly inconsolable, living in barely concealed dread, whilst Grandma Lizzie clutched at the old adage 'No news is good news'.

Since early September, when news had first been received that Harry was missing, Lizzie had written each month to the War Office seeking news. In November she had added Sam's name – pleading for any information at all about her boys, but nothing had been forthcoming. At last, on 25th January 1915, a postcard was received from Paderborn in Germany, where Harry was being held in a prison camp. He had been wounded and captured in the trenches near Mons and was now detained at the Kaiser's pleasure, along with a number of other Lostock boys, including his good pal, John Blane of Austin Street. Lizzie was encouraged. Not only was Harry obviously quite well, but, in fact, was something of his old, cheeky self in that he listed those items which would make his life as a P.O.W. more bearable. A parcel containing the requested cocoa, cake, syrup, socks and Woodbines was in the post within twenty four hours.

Early in April 1915, the grandparents in Ann Street gathered themselves in anticipation of the weekly visit from William's wife and their three young children. For an hour or so at least there would be an air of cheerfulness in the house. Absolute heartache followed. A special delivery had arrived. The children and their mother were distraught. Without speaking, Lizzie took the proffered letter, written by the Company Sergeant Major of 'B' Company, 1st Cheshire Regiment:

> Dear Mrs. Deakin,
> I am extremely sorry to be the bearer of bad tidings to your already troubled home and can honestly assure you that you have the most heartfelt sympathy of both the officers and men of 'B' Company in your great loss of which you will doubtless have been notified by now. In case you have not, I am sorry to say your husband was killed in action on the night of 12th March.
> It may be of some consolation to you to know he has been respectfully buried and a cross has been erected over his grave. The service was read by an Officer of our own Company.
> He was a most willing soldier, but not reckless; just the sort which we could ill-afford to lose. He died without a murmur of pain, just a true soldier's death. Please accept the sincere condolences of every man in the Battalion.
>   C.S.M.E. Owens
>   'B' Company, 1st Cheshires
> P.S. I got your address from a parcel which you had sent. The parcel was too broken up to return but the enclosed Postal Order is the 2s/6d you sent in it.

William's children needed comforting. They knew, simply, that their mother and grandmother were deeply distressed and, most surprisingly, even Granddad Sam had gone quietly to his bedroom. Within a few days Lizzie received the following letter from the War Office:

> Dear Mrs Deakin,
> In further reply to your enquiry of 14th February 1915, I am commanded by the Army Council to inform you that Regimental Number 9428 Corporal S. Deakin of the 1st Cheshire Regiment has now been reported in a casualty list

as missing since 21st October 1914. Further enquiries are being made and the result will be communicated to you in due course. This is the latest information regarding this soldier which has been received.

Two weeks later, Martha, Sam's young wife, arrived with her mother in support. She had received a letter from the War Office confirming that her beloved Sam, with whom she had enjoyed only a few months of married life, had been killed in action on 21st October 1914. For over seven long months the family had agonized over Sam's fate and now all hope was gone.

Sam Senior stared into the fire, a pose he would adopt frequently over the coming months. An over efficient local policeman might well have provided the final straw that broke Sam's emotional back. Living at Ann Street was Rex, a brown and white mongrel dog, who was slightly puzzled by the absence of his master, Harry. Police Constable Thomas had noticed the dog on Manchester Road and followed it home, where he had asked Lizzie for its licence. On being told that none existed, the policeman brought a prosecution despite being told that the dog belonged to a soldier in German hands. When the case came to the local court, Lizzie read a letter from Sam to the magistrates:

> Order of the Day
>
> It is my Royal and Imperial Command that you concentrate your energies, for the immediate present, upon one single purpose and that is that you address all of your skill and all the valour of my soldiers to exterminate first the treacherous English. Walk over General French's contemptible little army.
>
> Kaiser Wilhelm II. 19/8/14.
> German Army Headquarters. Aix-la-Chapelle
>
> *With huge irony, 'The Old Contemptibles' was the title proudly seized upon by men of the British Expeditionary Force who had seen service on or before 22nd November 1914. The medal which these troops were awarded was The 1914 Star (known as The Old Contemptibles Medal).*

> The dog belongs to my son who was taken prisoner of war at Mons in August 1914. We have another son who was killed at the Battle of Neuve Chappelle, whilst serving under Lieutenant Inman, and a third son killed in October 1914, who had been missing for over seven months. We have had so much to think about that we had forgotten to get a licence.

The Lost Boys of Lostock

The police prosecutor, an embarrassed Superintendent Ennion, immediately asked to withdraw the case, saying that if he had known the facts he would have helped Mr. Deakin to get a licence. He appreciated how much trouble the family had experienced. Within a few months the Deakin family were again in court – this time a Coroner's Court. A summary of the local newspaper's report on the case must suffice:

Samuel Alfred Deakin, aged 63, of Ann Street, committed suicide on the 16th December because of the deaths of his two sons and the capture of a third.

A daughter, Gladys, lived with her parents and said her dad had been in ill health for a considerable time. His foreman had sent him home last Thursday because he was rambling. He was permanently fretting over his sons but told the family he would be alright.

On Saturday morning, said his wife, Lizzie, he had eaten breakfast, then said he did not feel like work and had gone back to bed, while she had gone to market. When she returned Gladys told her that she had heard a sound like running water, had gone to the bedroom and found her father with blood running from his throat. Dr. Mainwaring-White had been sent for but it was too late as Sam had cut his jugular. The doctor said Sam was on the border of melancholia, but probably insane when he took his life.

George Hewitt said he had been Sam's foreman for years and he was an excellent cooper, but he had been depressed for some time, always troubling about his sons. He had been worried about Sam's mental state and sent him home in the care of a workmate.

Lizzie confirmed that they had no financial troubles. He often spoke about their boys and fretted over them, but he had never threatened to take his own life.

The jury reached the obvious verdict that Sam had committed suicide while insane with grief. The Coroner accepted the verdict and expressed great sympathy for the poor family.

In December 1918, Harry was repatriated. Lizzie's letters had reached him in Germany so he was aware of the great misfortunes which had befallen his family. Almost as an act of regeneration he was married to Mary Taylor within months and began his new life in Northwich. In 1926 he joined the newly-formed local branch of the Old Contemptibles Association. His brothers were gone but their glorious endeavours with the 1st Cheshires would occupy local soldiers' yarns throughout Harry's lifetime. Sadly, his brothers remained in France forever. Sam's body was lost in the trenches but he is commemorated on the memorial to over 13,000 men at Le Touret on the La Bassée road.

The battlefield grave of William survived the war and his remains were eventually moved to be buried along with nearly 400 other soldiers at Spoilbank Cemetery which is no more than three miles from Ypres town centre on the La Bassée road and no more than five miles from Sam's memorial.

The Connollys of Brook Street

IN 1895 William Connolly had moved his pregnant wife, Mary, and his infant sons, Thomas and John, from their first home in Runcorn to work as a bricklayer's labourer in the Brunner Mond Works at Lostock Gralam. Brook Street, just across the Manchester Road from the Works, was one of a series of small terraced streets built specifically to accommodate the workers and their families, essential to the production of salt in the Northwich area.

The Connollys settled at Number 16, enjoying the semi-rural lifestyle, as Thomas started at Lostock Infants' School. Young John delighted in being at home with Mum until the peace was rather shattered by the arrival of baby Leonard in March 1896. School represented an oasis of calm to John when he joined his elder brother in 1897. The older brothers became inseparable. Thomas walked John to and from school along the Manchester Road each day and, as the senior school was close by, continued this duty when he progressed to the august corridors of Lostock Gralam Boys' School in 1898. The Connolly influence in the Infant School was maintained, however, when Leonard took his brother's place in 1901: John being by now established in his personal paradise – the Big School – with Thomas.

At home, Mary's housekeeping burden had been added to by the arrival of Lily in 1901 and later in 1907, by the addition to the family of Doris. There was little spare money but the Connolly parents were careful and the family enjoyed a relatively comfortable existence. The three boys appear to have made solid progress at school, but their futures, as with the great majority of Lostock boys at the turn of the century, were destined to develop in the Salt Industry. First Thomas, in 1905, then John two years later and, finally, Leonard in 1910 made the quick crossing of Manchester Road into the Brunner Mond Works. The closeness of the older brothers can be traced throughout their teenage years as they worked, played (for the bowling club at Lostock Alkali) and socialised together. No doubt Nellie and Susie (who appear frequently in the post-war 'In Memoriam' columns) met the boys at the dances at the Lostock Pavilion, which served as the main community centre in the second decade of the twentieth century. John, closer in years to Leonard, joined the Gladstone Club in nearby Northwich with his younger brother.

At the outbreak of war in 1914, 23-year-old Thomas and John, aged 22, like so many young men of the day, saw a wonderful opportunity to engage in a great adventure, leaving Lostock Works and its salt pans far behind – at least until Christmas by which time the Huns would have been driven back into Germany. To date, the longest journey the boys had made had been from Runcorn to Lostock some twenty years earlier. Now the chance to visit mainland Europe presented itself and at no apparent cost to the family. Whilst feelings of patriotism predominated, Mary Connolly could not wholly share her husband's enthusiasm for their sons' project. Young Leonard envied his elder brothers' determination and regretted his youth – never more so than when they told the family, in August 1914, that they had enlisted, together as always, in the 12th Battalion of the Cheshire Regiment. They had attested, one behind the other, with John given the army number of 13900 and Thomas, 13901. Within days, the brothers had departed for Chester to join their new comrades in the 12th Cheshires (mainly men from the Stockport area) and to entrain for their first training camp in Seaford, Sussex. Leonard and the two little girls suddenly found that the house in Brook Street was quite a bit bigger than they had previously realised. Mary's washing and cooking burdens were considerably reduced and Lily found that she was significantly poorer as there were now no generous older brothers who, when they sank into their chairs after a hard shift at the Works, would pay a penny or so for her services in dashing to the local shop for a packet of Woodbines.

In the summer of 1915, after some ten months of training in and around the coast of Kent and Sussex, Thomas and John returned to Lostock on a two weeks' furlough. The family were delighted. Beds were readjusted and re-allocated and extra supplies of meat and vegetables purchased on Northwich market by the ever willing Mary, despite the protests of nine year old Doris, who grumbled quietly on the trek up Manchester Road with heavy shopping bags.

Christmas 1915 was enjoyed in the June of that year at 16, Brook Street. After a couple of days at home, the brothers broke the news that their leave meant that their training was almost complete. Soon they would sail for France. Mary was devastated. She was well aware of what was happening in Europe. Were not the photographs and obituaries of well-known faces starting to appear regularly in the Northwich Guardian?

The talk in the local shops was of those who had been wounded or taken prisoner at Mons. Sammy Whittaker, a workmate of the brothers, had been killed in the first week of the War; whilst the Deakin boys from nearby Ann Street, had suffered dreadfully. And now her boys were about to go to the front line!

The Connolly boys, l-r, Sgt.J.W.Connolly, Pte.T.H.Connolly, Pte.L.Connolly.

As they strode off on the short journey to Northwich station, Mary clutched Doris to her at the corner of Brook Street. Leonard and his Dad were in the Works, the former quiet and reflective, hoping that time would pass at twice its normal rate so that he could follow his brothers, whilst William told his mates, with barely concealed pride, that his boys and the lads from Stockport, who made up the 12th Cheshires, would soon sort out 'the bloody Huns'.

In the first week of September 1915, Thomas and John Connolly, proud of their standing in the Regiment, with a force of some 850 officers and other ranks, sailed from Folkestone to Boulogne; there they would join the 22nd Division. As the brothers leaned on the rail together, looking across to the slowly receding landfall, no doubt they talked of Lostock, the family and, above all, Nellie and Susie, who, on their last night together, had smiled with delight at that magical moment when the boys had produced engagement rings, and then sobbed on the realisation that Thomas and John would be leaving the next day. The farewells between the young couples that last night were tender and lingering. They were never to meet again!

The Channel crossing proved uneventful for the Battalion and they were soon settled in their camp just outside Flesselles in Northern France. Elsewhere, events were taking a turn that would significantly affect the lives of the brothers. In the Balkans, old and new enmities had once again been activated. Bulgaria was massing her armies on the borders of a weakened Serbia, who cried out to Britain and France for support. By October, the 12th Cheshires, as part of the 22nd Division, were on the move. They endured the long, uncomfortable train ride across France to Marseille, where they embarked at the end of October 1915 for Salonika in Greece, to join an Expeditionary Force and defeat the Serbs. However, they were too late and by the time they arrived the Bulgars were already established inside Serbia. To prevent future territorial ambitions of the Bulgarians, High Command decided to keep the force on the border 'twixt Greece and Serbia. As in France, huge defences were dug and so much barbed wire was laid some ten miles north of Salonika that the area was named 'The Birdcage'.

The next twelve months saw the 12th Cheshires engaged in one of the truly great stalemates of the War. They were surrounded on three sides by Bulgarian and German forces to such an extent that the Germans said that they had 'taken up residence in our concentration camp' (i.e. The Birdcage).

Back in England, stories were spread that the Force was in an 'easy' theatre of war, engaged in 'gardening duties'. Whilst there was truth in the suggestion that not as many bullets were flying about, the British troops had one very active enemy – the marsh mosquito which ensured that over 60% of the Macedonian force was laid low intermittently, for years to come, with malaria. The problem was exacerbated by the frequent non-arrival of essential supplies of quinine from the ships trying to reach Salonika but increasingly sent to the bottom of the Aegean Sea by German U-boat activity. The Connolly boys adopted a simple philosophy of 'needs must', found strength in each other's presence and simply got on with it. John's qualities indeed were soon recognized by his platoon commander and he quickly progressed through the ranks to win his sergeant's stripes. Thomas delighted in the success of his younger brother but never let him forget who enjoyed the real status on the family honours board. Apart from the odd night raid and an occasional artillery shell, life passed peacefully, if very uncomfortably, in Macedonia. Few men suffered at the hands of the enemy. Indeed the real killers were the mosquitoes and the influenza which was rampant amongst the British forces. Both Thomas and John had short spells in local hospitals but survived the ordeal.

In March 1916 John wrote to his local newspaper, the Northwich Guardian:

> I hope you will be able to give me space to thank the committee of the Lostock Mothers' Effort for the parcels sent to the Lostock lads. With me are T. Connolly, R. Cross and G. Hewitt, who all desire me to express their thanks for the gifts.

Mary and the girls would have been relieved and proud to see their brothers in the local press. Leonard's quiet envy would continue to develop. When would he be able to volunteer and do his bit?

In the summer of 1916 the 12th Cheshires were sent to the Lake Doiran front, some

60 miles north of Salonika. Otherwise, nothing much changed. The men were largely engaged in improving defensive positions, developing roads and building bridges. Generally conditions were appalling. After an unbearably hot summer they faced a bitterly cold winter. Supplies were poorer than ever as the U-boat campaign in the Aegean intensified. It was almost a relief when opposing troops again joined battle around the Bulgarian strong point known as the Grande Couronne – but the superb artillery observation post which the enemy had developed there was to bring catastrophe to the Connolly family.

Mary and William received a letter early in May 1917. It was signed by a platoon commander, Lieutenant R.S. Kay:

> On the night of April 25th Sergeant Connolly was in charge of a party carrying rations to the most advanced party of our newly captured line. They had nearly reached their objective when they came under heavy shellfire. Your son was rallying his men when a shell burst practically on top of him and a piece of shrapnel, hitting him in the back of his neck, killed him instantly.
> I cannot speak too highly of him, not only during recent operations, when his cheerful spirit, absolute disregard for danger and tactful power of command, proved him to be worth his very weight in gold, but also throughout the long and arduous campaign in this country.
> He was recognised by all as one of the very best N.C.O.s in the Battalion, but, however much we shall miss him, his loss, I know, is as nothing as it is to you. The whole Company sends its deepest sympathy and trusts that God may comfort you in your great loss.

Even worse was to follow. Within forty eight hours, a second letter arrived, signed by a Chaplain with the 12th Cheshires:

> I regret to inform you that your son, Sergeant J. Connolly, was killed instantly by a shell when going out with a working party and your other son, Private T. Connolly, was apparently caught and mortally wounded by another shell as he was returning to an advanced dressing station from the Regimental Aid Post where he had been classified as slightly wounded. Please accept the sincere condolences of all of the officers and men of the Battalion.

The sense of devastation at 16, Brook Street was palpable. At a stroke the eldest children, who had played, worked and fought together, had now died together. Leonard, who had finally enlisted two months before, was given a short, compassionate leave to be with the family but the war needed a regular supply of young men and he was under final training prior to his departure for France as a reserve with the South Lancashires, a territorial regiment whose personnel he had encountered during their guard duties at the very Brunner Mond Works he once entered daily. Mary's feelings can only be imagined as she watched him march off down Manchester Road. It had been less than two years ago that she had wept quietly as her eldest sons had stepped out on the same, short journey to Northwich station. Could any God allow the same cruel fate to take Leonard?

The Connolly family house, 16 Brook Street (left).

In July Leonard sailed, with the 1/4th South Lancashire Battalion, for France. As the winter of 1917 turned into spring he wrote home whenever possible, assuring the family that, although life was hard, he felt perfectly safe. On 22nd April a card arrived from Leonard saying that he had been wounded but that it was not too serious and there was nothing to worry about. Mary, however, harboured secret fears. She would not be really happy until her youngest son was home for good. Thus her joy, in August 1918, could hardly be contained. Leonard had suddenly arrived home for two weeks' furlough. He was thoroughly optimistic that the War would be over by Christmas and so the family should 'keep their chins up.' A quick round of visits followed to see those of his classmates who were home but who were too damaged to be going back to the War. Certainly he would be welcome at the Ainsworths' abode in Stanley Grove while Chris Johnson, who had been invalided home some two years before to 5, Brook Street, would make him more than welcome; and poor Sid Barber in Boundary Street was glad of visitors as he hated to be seen out as a one-legged cripple.

Life returned to normal at Number 16 when Leonard travelled back to the front. Mary felt a little more at ease. He had been his usual self, had assured her that he would soon be home for good and told his sisters what they could buy him for Christmas! Thomas and John had been remembered with great affection but . . . 'Next Year would see peace and the family would try to return to the comparative happiness of the pre-war years.'

Just two weeks after Leonard's visit, on Tuesday 10th September, a letter arrived from the Ward Sister at a Casualty Clearing Station in the Pas de Calais, Northern France:

> Your son, Private Leonard Connolly, was brought here on Thursday last, suffering from very severe wounds on both legs, one of which has had to be amputated and, I greatly fear he may have to lose the other.

Mary shook as she read. What terrible crime had she committed in the eyes of God that her family should be so punished?

On Monday 23rd the Sister wrote again:

> I regret very much to tell you the sad news that your son, Private L. Connolly, passed away last night, the 18th inst. He seemed to get on so well at first that we had every hope of his pulling through, but, of course, he was fighting against great odds.
> His two legs were so badly wounded that there was no alternative but to amputate them and he was so plucky about it all. I really do think it is better for him that it is so, for afterwards he would have felt the loss of his legs. He told me he had just come back from leave, so you have the comfort that you have seen him lately.

Mary's nightmares had found their own reality – all of her boys were gone. The house would never again resound to their jokes, their arguments and the preparations for the Saturday night dances as they disputed priority at the family sink. The girls sobbed. William stared into the grate. What was there left to say? The neighbours were kind. Martha Ainsworth at number 3 understood. She had lost her boy William two years before and her younger son Walter was ailing. Charlotte Buckley and Mary Ellen Faulkner regularly came to sit, to drink tea and to offer sympathy; both had lost sons in this bloody conflict. The Reverend Uttley from the Parish Church had visited to offer those condolences which he had offered to so many of his parishioners since August 1914. He asked Mary to bring the family to St. John's on Sunday where special prayers would be offered for all of the departed Lostock boys – especially those who had marched away from 16, Brook Street.

Some four years after the war, Mary and William received news of the final resting places of their sons and yet another family hope was dashed; Thomas and John were not lying next to each other as they had hoped. Thomas had been buried in the Doiran Military Cemetery whilst John had been laid to rest in the Karasoule Military Cemetery, some few miles away. Young Leonard was interred in the Pernes British Cemetery in Artois, but he is not alone as over one thousand of his fellow countrymen lie alongside him.

Life would never be the same again. Mary now had William, Lily and Doris to care for and her memories to treasure. The Connolly line was ended. William was the last male bearer of the name and soon, no doubt, Lily would be the first of the surviving girls to change her name – but it was not to be. Lily never married. Like so many of the daughters of that period she stayed at home. Then, at the age of twenty nine years she succumbed to influenza and, on 26th April 1930, the thirteenth anniversary of the deaths of her brothers in faraway Greece, she died.

That most dreadful of all occurrences, the death of a child before that of a parent, had been the fate of the Connollys four times. When William died in the April of 1932, only Doris remained to share Mary's grief.

How different was 16, Brook Street by the autumn of 1933. Whilst Mary had been able to conjure a display of happiness at the July wedding of twenty-six-year old Doris to Jack Wickers, a Northwich tinsmith, she was now alone with nothing but the ghostly echoes of her empty home; there she lived until she had her reunion with William, her boys and Lily in 1957 at the age of eighty seven years.

In Memoriam – Northwich Guardian, 19th September 1919.
To Pt. Thomas, Sgt. John and Pt. Leonard Connolly

We often think of days gone by
When we were all together.
A shadow on our lives is cast
Three loved ones gone forever.

Sadly missed – Father, Mother, Sisters and Susie
and Nellie (fiancées)'

The Terraced Rows

AS the nineteenth century reached its final decade the industrial development along the old Manchester Road from Northwich demanded homes for its workers. There was plenty of work available for the locals, too much in fact, in the salt industry and the Brunner Mond Works in Lostock Gralam.

Housing was at a premium in that largely rural landscape so a building programme was quickly instituted to provide the much needed accommodation. Within a three year period some one hundred new, terraced homes were built across seven streets, immediately opposite the main gates to Brunner's empire.

When the 1901 census was taken, the great majority of the houses were occupied but some few remained unfinished. By the summer of 1914, however, the entire 'estate' was complete and, indeed, some of the houses had already changed hands as the original occupants aspired to larger properties up on the main road. Individually the families were large – a majority numbering more than four children, most of whom, in 1901, were under ten years of age. By the Outbreak these boys were 'ready to do their bit'; many indeed would 'give their all'.

Half of the new houses were situated in Renshaw Street and Boundary Street (which remain, externally, surprisingly, untouched to this day) and still serve as depressing reminders of what the Great War meant to communities in small villages across Britain.

Renshaw Street
More than twenty-five men from the twenty-seven houses in Renshaw Street faced the guns of World War I, with more than one half of them wearing the insignia of the 10th Cheshires; five were to find their final resting place in France; of the remainder, over one half were to return physically scarred by battle for the rest of their lives.

No. 2: Myles and Nora Walsh had rented a shop on the corner of Manchester Road, just yards from their new home in Renshaw Street, so that they could provide a good selection of groceries for the locals and a reasonable standard of living for their young family. As the new century dawned, the Walshes, with their two young sons safely in the care of Nora's live-in sister, Margaret, worked hard at their business. Myles was quickly accepted as being a cut above the other rough and ready Irishmen working 'over the road' at Brunner's, but Nora was regarded with deeper suspicion, being from Knutsford and, in the opinion of some, having ideas above those of her neighbours, possibly because of her 'medical background.'

In fact Nora, before her marriage, had been in service as a housemaid in the prestigious King Street, Knutsford home of a prominent Manchester physician and surgeon, Mr John T. Appleby. It is reasonable to believe that this insight into that middle class lifestyle had planted the seed of ambition within her. Furthermore, she had observed her Irish immigrant parents, who had progressed from work as labourers on a farm in Plumley, to owning a small greengrocery in Market Place, Knutsford.

Her children would have a better start in life and, at the age of seven, in his Sunday-best clothes, young Richard was escorted by his mother to Stockton Heath, some eight miles away. Nora had seen the advertisements in the Northwich Guardian for Woods Tutorial College, which offered the finest schooling possible for boys from good homes – at a price! All-persuasive, of course, was the fact that the headmaster personally conducted the admission interviews 'in his private residence'. A combination of young Richard's demeanour and the proceeds from his parents' cash till, ensured that the next four years would be spent under the careful supervision of Mr Woods at a monthly cost of seventeen shillings and sixpence. In 1910 the daily grind of the journey to Stockton Heath came to a merciful end when Richard, to his mother's unbridled joy, won a place at Sir John Deane's Grammar School in Northwich, where he was to pass a pleasant five years until he secured an apprenticeship in the Brunner Mond laboratories.

At the Outbreak Richard watched as many of his older neighbours marched away. Eventually, in April 1917, despite Nora's anguished protests, Richard visited the local recruiting office, enlisted for General Service and was posted to the 1st Battalion of the South Wales Borderers, a regular force which had suffered heavily since their arrival in France in August 1914. Richard's war lasted but seven months when Mrs Harper came to the shop one dreary November morning; Nora asked Myles to hold the fort whilst she took the lady to the comfort of the back room. But muffled screams were to come from Nora's mouth as she received the news that had somehow become inevitable. William Harper had written home from the front to tell his mother that Richard Walsh had been killed in action during a raid on German trenches near Passchendaele, a fact confirmed by an official telegram in early December.

Richard's battlefield grave was lost in the fighting of Spring 1918 but his name is commemorated forever on the Tyne Cot Memorial, which bears the names of nearly 35,000 men who have no known grave. Perhaps the family's loss can best be summed up by a letter, dated 30th June 1922, in which the Officer in charge of Military Records requests permission from the Ministry of War to dispose of Richard's unclaimed medals. Richard, of whom so much was expected, was no more. What point in medals?

No. 4: Next door, young Lizzie Adamson quietly sobbed as the news of Rick Walsh's death spread along the street. It was only a year ago that she had experienced the despair that Nora and her family were now suffering and the wounds remained open. John Adamson was born in nearby Peover in 1889. His dad ran the local pub but, as his family grew, he decided that the salt pans offered a better wage and, by the turn of the century, had moved his wife and five children to Fitton Street in Lostock Gralam. On leaving the local school Jack, like so many of his peers, joined the daily trek to Brunner's, played for the works bowling team and rarely missed his weekly visit to St. John's Church. His steady routine was rudely interrupted by the late summer news from the Balkans and, on the first of September 1914, Jack joined a number of his Brunner mates on the walk to the Northwich recruiting office and, by the time he arrived home, he was a member of the 10th Battalion of the Cheshires. His fiancée, Lizzie Bloor, was not de-

A group of Cheshires in training.

lighted at the news but – it was what patriotic young men were doing and she would not want her Jack to be different. In early 1915, household matters came to a head. Lizzie, working in domestic service in Altrincham, wrote to Jack with news of a super little house available in Renshaw Street, which, as a Brunner Mond man, he could rent. Next home leave, in April 1915, the pair were married at Dunham Chapel near Altrincham and quickly set up their first home at Number 4 before Jack rejoined his unit.

The 10th Cheshires moved to France in September 1915. Jack's embarkation leave was a poignant occasion but he assured Lizzie that he would be back to celebrate Christmas with her. However he was to spend that particular festival in a field ambulance with a bout of sickness. That spring his letters home were full of optimism. There was talk in the ranks of a 'big push' coming in the summer that would see to the Fritzes once and for all. It was just a matter of time before they could really be husband and wife. How hollow that forecast seemed when Lizzie received the news that Jack was 'missing presumed wounded' in late July.

The 10th Cheshires had indeed been involved in the push on the Somme. Jack's company, having spent ten days defending the trenches near the village of Ovillers, attacked at 5.30am. on the 14th July in divisional formation, at Bazentin. Disaster followed. The men were driven back by withering German machine gun fire and then, in the illusory safety of their own trench, they suffered a hail of heavy artillery fire which almost obliterated the Battalion. Jack Adamson simply disappeared, as did many of his mates, and only fragmented body parts remained. For this reason his death could not be established and Lizzie was made to wait in fearful hope that Jack might just 'turn up', possibly as a prisoner. A letter of confirmation arrived in early December. Jack was presumed to have been killed in the action of 14th July and, after a marriage of only eighteen months, another young widow was left to question her faith. Lizzie survived the paperwork from the military and, in July, was awarded a pension of thirteen shillings and ninepence per week, but only after some rather sinister comments were written on the official documentation about her marriage having occurred 'after enlistment'.

Over 75,000 men are commemorated on the huge Thiepval Memorial to the Missing of the Somme, some 65,000 having died in the 144 days between 1st July and 14th November 1916; amongst them is Jack Adamson.

One of a series of annually published tributes to Jack that appeared in the local newspaper each July from 1917:

Fondly I loved him, he is dear to me still,
But in grief I must bend to my God's holy will.
My sorrow is great, my loss hard to bear,
But angels, dear Jack, will guard you with care.'
Never forgotten by your loving wife, Lizzie.

No. 7: Just across the street, at number 7, lived Thornton and Mary Jane (née Finlay) Hickson. Married in the parish church in August 1911, they had set up home in a truly convenient location, directly over the road from Thornton's job at the Works and, even better, a mere hundred yards' walk from Mary Jane's former family home in Boundary Street. An added bonus was that Thornton's best friend, James Finlay, one of his wife's five brothers, still lived there. The link between the Hickson – Finlay families was strengthened in August 1913 when Florence Hickson married Richard Finlay

The Thiepval Memorial on which is inscribed the names of over 75,000 men killed in the Somme battles.

and even further cemented when James Finlay, along with his new wife, Margaret (née Gough) were given accommodation at No.7. This arrangement, however, was to have a poignant twist when Margaret died soon after giving birth to Maud Dora, although Mary Jane and Thornton were delighted to be able to adopt the baby.

Fired with patriotic enthusiasm, Thornton enlisted into the 10th Cheshires on 1st September 1914. He appears to have been a good soldier, the only stain on his record being seven days confined to barracks for overstaying his leave period at Renshaw Street by a few days. Along with his mates, he left for France in September 1915, his first battle destined to be on the Somme the following July. Thornton was, however, to miss the carnage of the first day of the battle as he was convalescing in the military hospital at Étaples, having been badly wounded in the neck and thigh by gun and shell fire during trench-fighting in early June. In late July he had rejoined his old pals in the 10th Cheshires and, just before the end of the year, was able to write home that he had met 'Little Joe', the youngest of the Finlay boys in rest camp.

By now, Thornton was wearing a lance corporal's stripe, awarded to him in October 1916. As the hostilities on the Somme ground to a halt in the rain and cloying mud of late November, it seemed perhaps that a more hopeful New Year lay ahead. High Command would soon render any such dreams futile. On 17th September 1917, Thornton was one of over two hundred 10th Cheshires who waited in their trenches at 10.30am to allow the British artillery to do its work on the German trenches near Romarin, essentially to shatter the barbed wire entanglements and also to demoralize the German defenders. In reality it did neither. Eventually the men, mainly from Northwich and Lostock, attacked across no man's land, but, despite some initial gains won by a combination of sheer doggedness and naked bravery, the Cheshires were driven back. Approximately one hundred of them were casualties, some forty being dead; amongst them was Thornton Llewellyn Hickson.

After the official letter and whilst still suffering from shock, Mary Jane received a visitor, Bob Simpson, a comrade of Thornton's. Having handed her his wallet, papers and photographs, he related how he had attacked alongside her husband on the 17th, had witnessed his being wounded in the wrist and had shouted to him to go back for treatment. In the flush of the charge Thornton had refused, pushed forward and had been killed almost immediately by a shell.

In the aftermath of battle, the remains of many of the men who had died on that day could not be identified. Their sacrifice is recorded, along with the names of 11,000 other allied troops killed in this sector, on the Ploegsteert Memorial.

Mary Jane and Maud Dora were given a pension of eighteen shillings and ninepence per week as compensation. Within eighteen months, in August 1918, almost seven years to the day since her wedding, Mary Jane's father, James Finlay, told the Coroner that the day after Bob Simpson's visit, she had taken to her bed and had been ill at regular intervals ever since. Thornton's sister, Florence, told how Mary Jane had collapsed and died in her arms. Dr. Doonan said that the post mortem had revealed that she had died of an enlarged heart – but the family were convinced that the real cause lay on a French battlefield.

No. 18: The newly formed Dufficey family had moved from Runcorn to 5, Renshaw Street in 1901, just after Mary Thompson had merged her family of five with Frank Dufficey's four offspring.

Joseph was Mary's eldest son and, on leaving school in 1906, he began work on a local farm where he was to be found at the Outbreak in 1914. Along with his great pal from Number 18, Sam Hitchen, Joseph had enlisted in the Cheshires but, before the completion of his training, he had accepted a transfer to the 7th Battalion of the Queen's Own Royal West Kent Regiment. Wounded in the fighting on the Somme, Joseph had been granted furlough at home and, seizing the opportunity, had married Edith Hitchen, Sam's sister, and enjoyed a brief honeymoon in his new home at Number 18, the Hitchen residence.

Pte.R.Walsh, Pte.J.Adamson, Pte.J.Kelly.

The West Kents was a regiment that had suffered enormous losses during the war and front-line reinforcements were a regular requirement. In the German advance, in the spring of 1918, the 7th Battalion especially had brought great credit upon themselves in the rearguard action until in early April, they were withdrawn from the line and allowed to recuperate and reform a few miles from Villers-Bretonneux at St. Fuscien.

On April 24th, at 6.00am, the Battalion left the comparative comfort of their rest camp and manned the trenches on the road between Cachy and Domant, facing Hangard Wood, supporting a large detachment of Australian troops bent on halting the German advance. At 10.00pm, the 480 men of the Battalion were ordered to go 'over the top'. Despite being faced by withering machine gun fire, the men were initially successful and fierce, hand-to-hand fighting followed in the German trenches. The Australians were even more successful and managed to lay siege to the town of Villers-Bretonneux.

Only 253 men answered the 7th Battalion roll call on the 25th April. When Joseph Thompson's name was called, there was no response. Indeed Joseph was gone forever, his body never having been found. Whilst many of his mates are buried in Hangard Wood Cemetery, a large number of them, like Joseph, have no known grave and are commemorated on the great Pozieres Memorial, which lists the names of over 14,000 soldiers lost in the fighting between March and August 1918.

No. 22:
During the whole of the morning our own artillery fired short into my front line. Despite my continually reporting this matter the short shooting continued resulting in a large portion of the front line . . being knocked in, causing me many casualties.
At 2.00pm enemy artillery opened up with a terrific barrage of heavies on our wire, front and trenches. This was kept up until 3.15pm when he attacked vigorously in large numbers in four waves.
The attack completely broke under our intense rifle and Lewis gun fire and not a single man reached our wire.'
EXTRACT 'War Diary 10th Cheshires' 23rd March 1918

Jack Kelly was typical of many of the Lostock boys who had enlisted in August 1914 in the 10th Cheshires. He had been born, like many of them, outside the village – in his case to Irish immigrant parents – in Flint, North Wales. Jack's dad, James, had lost his first wife, Ellen, mother of his three daughters, in 1884; he had also 'lost' thirteen years off his age before the 1887 acquisition of his second wife, Martha, who presented him with Eleanor in 1888 and John George (always known as Jack) in 1892.

The family joined the growing community in Lostock in the mid-1890s when James, now in his early 60s, started at Brunners. Jack was enrolled at St. Wilfrid's Catholic Infant School and Martha established a home at the newly-built house in Renshaw Street. Jack's rather sober childhood, influenced by a father approaching his seventies and also by older sisters, was rescued somewhat when he started work at Brunners on the same day as another school leaver, John Bladon, of Station Road. Their friendship, which started that day in 1906, was to end on 23rd March 1918 when they were killed in different sectors of the same battlefield. The two boys quickly won places in one of the Works' Bowling teams and, by 1914, were playing regularly for the newly-established

Lostock Rovers Football Club. By the Outbreak the boys were inseparable and, along with a large number of their pals, they soon enlisted and were posted to the 10th Cheshires. Jack endured the training with only two minor skirmishes with the military authorities: one when he lit a surreptitious cigarette on a route march through the Wiltshire countryside; another when, more significantly, he overstayed his embarkation leave by a dastardly ninety minutes!! Each time he received three days 'Confined to Barracks'.

The 10th Cheshires, after a period of acclimatization, arrived in the Front Line trenches on 17th May 1916. They were immediately involved in some fierce hand-to-hand fighting and Jack, within days, found himself out of action with a gunshot wound to his hand. Jack survived the slaughter on the Somme in 1916 and the carnage around Ypres in 1917. There was great delight in Renshaw Street when he arrived home on New Year's Eve 1917 for a two week furlough – but his now-widowed Mum's anxiety on his return to the front on 12th January 1918 was to be realised when the Battalion Chaplain's letter arrived in early April:

> The news of your sad loss by the death of your son has no doubt reached you. He was killed in action whilst serving as a stretcher bearer on 23rd March. The Commanding Officer, Lt. Colonel Williams, desires me to write to you to express his sincere feelings at this time. It is a blow to us all and we feel it intensely.

Later that day the mother of Harry Boden, a Northwich boy, arrived at Number 22 to share both her grief and a letter which she had received from another son, George :

> There were two stretcher bearers killed whilst carrying our Harry out and saving his life. One of them was a chap called Jack Kelly from Lostock.

Jack had died a hero: killed by shellfire, possibly from his own artillery. His body was never found and his death is commemorated on both the Arras Memorial and on the family headstone in St. John's Churchyard, Lostock.

No. 1: George Lamb, born in 1892, joined the Cheshires at the Outbreak and survived unscathed until March 1918 when he was captured. Within two weeks, along with eleven comrades, he succeeded in escaping from his prison camp, was slightly wounded in the later stages of the conflict, but survived to reunite with his brother, Albert Lamb, by six years George's junior, who had also fought with the Cheshires and had received five gunshot and shrapnel wounds in his two years of service with the colours. He, too, survived the war to return to the family home and another reunion with the youngest brother, Henry, who because of his age, had been the last of the brothers to enlist, in May 1917. He had been rushed to the front with his Manchester Regiment mates in June 1918. Within two short months he was back home in England, lying in Hendon Military Hospital severely wounded in both his legs, his war over. The Lamb brothers returned to Lostock, damaged, but able to resume their duties, both at Brunners and in the local Boy Scout movement.

No. 6: On 7th September 1914, John Routledge wrote to his wife from his billet with the 1st Cheshires, a mere 20 miles from Paris, where the first German advances had been halted:

> I am still alive and in good health, but only by the mercy of God and your prayers. I have been in two big battles, but have managed to come out alive. It is a miracle how I have been saved, but I have had good faith in myself from the start and I have prayed to God to preserve and keep me safe to the end.
> The Germans are suffering terrible losses and by the time you receive this letter the war will be almost over. I hope and trust that I shall pull through now, being as we have, I feel, stood the hardest part of it.
> I should like to tell you more but we are afraid of German spies getting hold of our letters still, I would like to tell you what I have experienced since I have been out here, but I hope it won't be long before I get home to you. It is a pleasure to think of home after what we have gone through here. I will not write more now but will let you have another letter before long. I am sorry to keep you so long without a letter but I have had a hard job to write this.
> Give my best wishes to those who remember me in good old Lostock.
> Keep your heart up for I am nearly sure that it won't last much longer.

John had been one of the Old Contemptibles, landing in France on 16th August 1914 and managing to survive those early battles at Mons and La Bassée, which had devastated the ranks of the 1st Cheshires. His luck was to run out on 5th November 1914 when, in the first Battle at Ypres, he was captured and his war ended in Munsterlager prison camp in Hanover, Germany, along with Joe MacDonald of Boundary Street and a number of other local boys. Whilst there, John managed to send letters to his wife, Bedelia, who sent food parcels in return. Despite a serious bout of pneumonia, John made a safe journey home by Christmas 1918 – exactly as he had forecast – but four years late.

No. 13: A porter for Great Central Railway, Alfred Cross was to leave his post for a mere two months after enlisting into the 10th Cheshires on 1st September 1914. He joined the Battalion in their training camp at Codford, Wiltshire, but, on 4th November, returned home, permanently discharged as being medically unfit for future military service.

No. 19: Medals won by Sam Harvey in 1917 were the highest awards made to any of the men of Lostock Gralam. Sam's family had moved to Renshaw Street from Frodsham at the century's turn and, at the earliest opportunity, he had enlisted in the 1st Cheshires. As a reservist he had been called to accompany the Expeditionary Force's landing in France in August 1914. Sam survived the travails of major conflagrations until, as a battle-hardened sergeant, he was awarded both a D.C.M. and, most unusually, a French Military Medal for:

> Persistently performing good works and at all times setting a splendid example.

On 14th May 1917, with Sarah, his recently widowed mum, watching, Sam was decorated by King George V at Chester Castle. Sam's younger brother, Joe, wounded in the foot on the Somme with the 10th Cheshires in October 1916, had been hugely disappointed at being unable to see Sam receive his awards. He had been recuperating from his wounds at home but had been forced to return to the Front the day before the Chester ceremony. Brother George had been a 3rd Cheshires regular until, in 1909, he had been discharged to allow him to join the Royal Navy. All three brothers survived the war.

No. 27: The six Cross brothers had all enlisted within six weeks of the Outbreak. Three of them, Thomas, John and Frank, appear to have survived the war relatively unscathed. George, of the 3rd Rifle Brigade, had been quite seriously gassed in April 1915, outside Ypres and, despite spending some four months in hospital, he was discharged as being no longer fit for military service in the August of that year. On his discharge form his Commanding Officer rated him 'a very good hard-working man.'

His younger brother, William, who had arrived in France with the 8th South Lancashires in September 1915, survived many of the great battles, but, in 1918, on June 1st he was captured in a trench raid and spent the remainder of the war as a prisoner.

Robert Cross spent the war in Salonika with the 12th Cheshires, paying regular visits to both field and general hospitals whilst there, suffering from a variety of illnesses endured by many of the men engaged in that theatre. He was regularly struck down by malaria and chronic eye problems, including corneal ulcers. However, his service was still highly commended by his Commanding Officer, Lieutenant Colonel Watson, who wrote, *'He is a very smart soldier and is very reliable in his work.'*

By the spring of 1919, Renshaw Street had returned, as close as it would ever return, to its pre-war state. Five of its sons had been killed and at least another twelve would remain damaged for the rest of their days.

Boundary Street

No. 8: The War Diary of the 1st.. Battalion Cheshire Regiment records, on 28th August 1916, that Second Lieutenant C.V. Blain joined 'B' Company as a reinforcement just as they were heading for the front line near Leuze Wood, outside Guillemont in the Somme sector. Within three days, Charles Blain led his first patrol to clear out a German machine gun pit entrenched near Falfemont Farm, succeeded in the venture and returned unscathed. Two days later, on September 3rd, Charles again led his platoon in a major attack across the same ground and, within minutes of going 'over the top', lay mortally wounded in a shell hole.

Charles Victor Blain had been in France a mere ten days.

Over the Top.

Born in Northwich in 1888 to Charles senior, a stone mason, and Annie Blain, young Charles had moved, on the death of his father and subsequent re-marriage of his mother, to Number 8 Boundary Street in 1900. His step-father, James Butterworth, a clerk in the chemical works, was a man of some fortitude, embracing as he did, a woman some ten years his senior and her family of five sons and three daughters.

On leaving school, Charles was employed as an ironmonger's assistant, graduating to shop manager before joining the 3rd Cheshires, a battalion permanently based near Birkenhead as part of the Mersey Defences, guarding the Docks either side of the river. Charles had prospered and, by early 1916, had achieved the acting rank of Company Sergeant Major. However, the action for which so many young men yearned lay across the Channel and, having accepted the offer of officer training, he returned to Lostock on embarkation leave, proudly bearing the insignia of a Second Lieutenant, before beginning his final journey. He was destined to join his new battalion, the 1st Cheshires, which was desperate for reinforcements after its travails in and around Delville Wood. Many young subalterns had been lost and Charles knew he would be filling 'a dead man's boots.'

Charles Victor Blain now lies in Flatiron Copse Cemetery, alongside Mametz Wood. He is also remembered on the small war memorial in Comberbach village where his mother had moved in 1920.

No. 22: John Buckley was the eldest child and, therefore, principal supporter to his widowed mother, Charlotte, and his four siblings. After leaving Lostock Boys' School in 1908 he had joined the morning march to Brunner Mond, working as a labourer in the salt pans. His weekends were mainly spent playing bowls and football for the various area teams, but he dedicated many of his evenings to the local branch of the St. John's Ambulance Brigade. At the Outbreak, John had accompanied many of his pals, enlisted in the 10th Cheshires and followed the well-trodden route through training to the embarkation port of Folkestone in September 1915.

John's front line fighting involvement was relatively brief. He had sampled trench warfare in May 1916, during which nearly one third of his battalion were made casualties, mainly by shell fire. These numbers, however, almost pale into insignificance when compared with those emanating from the fighting in the first two weeks of July when the men found themselves in the trenches outside Ovillers:-

> WAR DIARY 14.07.16: At 11.00pm we attacked ... We actually got into the enemy trenches in places only to be driven back by intense machine gun fire. By 2.00am we had re-organised and, with the assistance of the 11th Lancs. Fusiliers we again attacked at the point of the bayonet but were again driven back by machine gun fire and suffered very heavy casualties.

John William Buckley was one of the men who fell that night. For some days he was listed as 'missing, presumed killed' but he never reappeared and his body was lost to the battlefields. He is one of more than 72,000 men commemorated on the Thiepval Memorial.

No. 23: In the major offensive towards Passchendaele in October 1917, the 3rd Australian Division succeeded in capturing the huge barn, named by the Northumberland Fusiliers as 'Tyne Cottage', which protected six German block houses, or 'pill boxes'. One of these was so large that it was immediately used as an advanced dressing station, where front line troops could receive prompt treatment. Those who did not survive were buried close by – hence Tyne Cot cemetery was established.

After the Armistice, remains were brought in from many of the nearby battlefields and, by the time of George V's visit in 1922, the largest Commonwealth War Cemetery in the world had been established. Over 35,000 men with no known grave were commemorated on the great memorial whilst, in the burial ground, lie a further 12,000 of whom only 3,600 are under named headstones. One of these is John Thomas Faulkner, aged 19 years, of the 2/9th Battalion Manchester Regiment. John was sixteen years of age when his mates from Brunner marched away, mainly to join the 10th Cheshires, in August 1914. As the eldest of six children, he was obliged to contribute to the family finances but, no doubt fired by younger brother William's thwarted enlistment, aged 15, in 1915, John joined up in May 1916 and was posted to the 2/9th Manchesters, originally formed as a reserve unit, which would train troops for other Manchester battalions. Casualties, however, being so high, the 2/9ths were sent to France as a combat force in March 1917. With the carnage around Ypres that summer, John and his pals were sent to the front, finally arriving in the rain-soaked, mud-covered, jumping-off trenches barely thirty minutes before the attack was launched, at 5.30am, on the village of Poelcapelle. The date was 9th October 1917.

The Lost Boys of Lostock

> The Manchesters, as part of the 66th Division 'had never been in battle before and had moved forward under the impression that they were going in to support. Without food or water for twenty-four hours, the division arrived so late on the battlefield that the covering barrage had to be brought back. Since the gunners were not in direct contact with the front line, they opened fire on their own men and cut the 66th to pieces.
>
> 'Haig's Command' – Denis Winter

What was left of them ran straight into withering machine gun and sniper fire. Despite the appalling mud and incessant shell fire some progress was made until, totally exhausted, they were forced to withdraw. In that single day's fighting, 3,120 men from the 66th (2nd East Lancashire) Division were casualties, over 120 of them being from the 800 men of John Faulkner's battalion.

Records show that many of those six score were, like John, mere boys of 19 and 20 years of age experiencing their very first battle.

No. 25: James and Sarah MacDonald had 'followed the Salt Trail' from Runcorn, via Middlewich, to Lostock Gralam at the turn of the century. They were the first occu-

A well-earned rest in the Trenches.

pants of their Boundary Street home on its completion in 1908, by which time their family of five boys and two girls were already starting to go their own way. Harry, the eldest child, had recently married, whilst Joseph, second in line, had enlisted in the regular army, as an eighteen year old, in 1904. Archibald had tried to enlist too, in 1907, but had been rejected because of the appalling condition of his teeth. However, his dental agonies became less of a problem with the Outbreak. As a serving soldier in the 1st Cheshires, Joseph was sent, on 16th August 1914, as part of the 'Contemptible Little Army', to defend Belgium against the German Army. Like so many of his mates, he was declared 'missing' at Mons, only to write home some weeks later from his new residence in a prison camp at Münster, in Westphalia; here he was to remain, regularly complaining in his infrequent letters home, of the boredom and lack of food, until his repatriation on Christmas Eve 1918. Archibald's teeth had passed the less than stringent examination in force in early September 1914 and he was assigned to the 10th Cheshires (whose twelve month training period is reported on elsewhere in this volume.) Archibald was no shrinking violet and his military trainers were soon trying to keep him to the straight and narrow, a task rendered almost impossible by the availability of cheap alcohol. His service record shows that on at least three occasions before the 10th Cheshires sailed for France in September 1915, Archibald had already faced three separate charges for drunken behaviour, the most serious being that he had used 'obscene and threatening language to an N.C.O.' An old enemy was to concentrate Archibald's mind wonderfully towards the end of that year, however, when he had to report on a number of occasions to the Field Ambulance, plagued by the pain from his crumbling teeth.

The 10th Cheshires experienced the front line for the first time on 17th May 1916 when they were assigned trenches facing Vimy Ridge. Four days later, at 5.00am, the Germans launched a six hour artillery bombardment on one sector, paused for four hours and then, at 3.00pm, re-launched a major artillery attack.

> It was without doubt, the heaviest, concentrated shelling of the war so far; the enemy had arrayed some 80 batteries on a 1,800 yard front ... 70,000 shells fell in four hours, flattening trenches and cutting all communications ... At 7.45pm the blowing of a huge German mine signalled the beginning of their infantry attack.
>
> Chris Baker - the long,long,trail

Archibald lost his life, as did some seventy-five other 10th Cheshires in the carnage. Exactly one week later a letter arrived at No. 25:

> Dear Mr MacDonald,
> I regret to inform you that your son was reported missing on the 21st but I fear there is very little hope of his ever being seen alive again. Should I hear anything of him I will at once write to you.
> I desire to express my deepest sympathy with you in the suspense and sorrow this note may bring.
> Yours sincerely,
Rev. D. Tait Patterson

His body was never found and he is commemorated on the Loos Memorial.

No. 26: The Johnsons were a well-established Northwich family when their son, John, took Clara as his bride and brought her to the family home at Edward Street. John's work at Brunner's however, soon enabled him to rent one of the newly built properties in Boundary Street and, by 1914, their roots were firmly established, with their six children, at No. 26. Harry (christened Henry), aged 16, was the eldest of three boys, whilst Florence, aged 11, led the girls. As was normal Harry followed his dad to Brunner's and, consequently, further developed his friendship, established at infant school, with John Faulkner, who lived just across the road at No.23.

No. 23: The boys enlisted within days of each other in May 1916, but had signed for General Service, hence, for the first time in over twelve years, they were to be separated – John being assigned to the Manchesters and Harry, at first, to the Cheshires. However, when recruits were sought to fill the depleted ranks of the Royal Warwicks at the Front, Harry immediately volunteered in the hope of meeting up with his pal, whom he knew was 'somewhere in France'. The devastating news of John's death at Poelcapelle in October 1917 left both families in deep shock but worse was to follow. In the spring of 1918, the German Army launched its great counter-attacks and, in the fighting near Estaires on the River Lys, Harry Johnson was killed in action on 9th April 1918. Just as his friend John Faulkner, Harry's body was never found and he is commemorated on the great Pozières Memorial along with a number of his mates from the 2/6th Royal Warwicks.

Both families had lost their eldest child.

The Lost Boys of Lostock

No. 28: Henry Postles was only one year old when his Dad, Thomas, died at the young age of 26, whilst working in the salt works at Runcorn. His Mum, Mary Ann, faced with the grim prospect of bringing up Henry (Harry to his family and the world at large) and his two older brothers, Thomas (4) and Joseph (2) was offered assistance in her task in the form of Joe Eaton, a labouring colleague of her late husband's. By 1900 the Eatons had produced four more children and had moved to Northwich following the 'salt trail'.

On leaving school in 1906, Harry was apprenticed at Broady's Gentlemen's Tailors; but, on the family's move to Boundary Street, the lure of higher wages and the camaraderie available at Brunner's, just across the Manchester Road, led Harry to join his step-dad. Like so many young men of his day he showed great interest in football and by 1910 was a regular for the village team, Lostock Gralam Football Club. Furthermore, a smart uniform and regular weekend camps enticed him, in 1909, into the local 'Terriers', the 5th Earl of Chester's Battalion. At the Outbreak Harry's training was quickly progressed and, after a final two weeks' leave, he was to rejoin the regiment for transportation to France. Mary Ann, still grieving at the loss of her second husband in a works accident, was deeply saddened when Harry took his final leave of her and his four younger siblings. But, all of his training had led to this moment so the only option for her was the 'brave face'.

At the end of January 1915, Harry left Boundary Street for the last time to return to his camp at Northampton and, on 15th February, he sailed with the 1/5th Cheshires (the number 1 indicating the territorial status of the battalion). They disembarked at Le Havre, where, after a short period of acclimatization, they gathered necessary supplies and set out for the front line trenches near Ypres at Neuve Chapelle. Harry's first duty was to write to his Mum to tell her of his safe arrival; his second letter, sent on 9th March, told her of his survival 'without a scratch'; the third letter wasn't from Harry but from Sam Hunter, a pal of his, who wrote to Mary Ann to give her the dreadful news. They had been sharing a trench on the night of 27th March when a heavy artillery attack had started. Harry had felt that the trench in front offered better protection so had attempted to crawl over the battered parapet into the slightly more comfortable offerings ahead. No sooner had his torso risen above the ground when two snipers' bullets caught him, one in the chest, the other in the head. Harry was dead before his body hit the ground. His visit to France had lasted just six weeks.

Harry's remains lie in the Kemmel Château Military Cemetery, some 5 miles from

Ypres. This young man of 'bright and cheerful disposition', according to the letter of sympathy from the battalion padre, was just over 22 years of age.

No. 6: The older children of the Barber family had moved into Boundary Street in unusual circumstances. Their parents, Tom and Elizabeth, had separated in 1912 after a marriage which had lasted some 28 years and produced ten children including twin sons, Sydney and Frank, born in 1893. They, with their younger brother, Harold, had all found employment at Brunner's as Iron Hamper Makers after leaving Lostock Boys' School. At the Outbreak, the twins had 'joined the crowd' and enlisted on 1st September in the 10th Cheshires and, until June 1917, they shared the same history. Then, on

German trench at Ypres.

10th June, during the 25th Division's attack on the Messines Ridge, Sydney was hit by a bullet and removed to the Field Ambulance. However, within three weeks, he was back with his unit, fighting just outside Ypres. Sadly, after a period of rest behind the lines, the 10th Cheshires were ordered to the front line trenches on 30th August 1917. Here, Sydney's war was to be ended by a heavy artillery shell blast which shattered his left leg and killed a number of his mates. Frank survived the battle unscathed and went on to fight at St. Quentin before his battalion was engaged in the huge conflagration at Bapaume in late March 1918. When the roll was called, Frank was missing and his pal, George Riley, from Northwich, wrote to his Mum that he thought Frank had been killed.

Mrs Riley passed the letter to the Barber family who were inconsolable at the loss of their brother, particularly as his twin was now home albeit permanently crippled.

Within ten days, glorious news arrived - Frank was safe! He had merely become detached from his platoon during the smoke of battle. He went on to complete his service, picking up a Military Medal for bravery on the way, and rejoined his twin in November 1918. Awaiting their reunion was young Harold, who had enlisted in the Cheshires in March 1917, but had never left England. After a few months he had been discharged from future military service because of a disordered action of the heart. The Barbers were, generally speaking, intact and Sydney had a rather unusual pension awarded to him to commence on 8th September 1918. He would have £1.7s.6d. per week for nine weeks which would then reduce to 16s.6d. per week. One wonders what physical improvement Sydney was likely to make in that short period!!

No. 12: Immediately on reaching his fourteenth birthday in June 1914, Joseph Finlay had taken his normal line of action – following his older brothers, James and Richard, firstly into an apprenticeship as an Iron Hamper Maker at the Union Acid Company, and then into the Territorials. Because of his youth, Joseph had been assigned to the 2/5th Cheshires, a Home Defence battalion, which would be permanently stationed in the United Kingdom. Whilst this suited him until he reached his majority, Joseph then asked to be transferred into a regiment of the line where action, by 1916, was more than guaranteed. His wish was granted and the 1st Battalion of the Loyal North Lancs. Regiment could soon count a new enthusiast on its manifest. Despite being wounded at the second battle of Passchendaele in early November 1917, Joseph survived the war with his officers noting his ability as a bomb thrower. Indeed, in April 1918 at a regimental parade just after the battle of Bethune, his bravery on the battlefield won him a Distinguished Conduct Medal, making him the most highly decorated Lostock Gralam boy of the war.

No. 14: Like so many of his contemporaries, 18-year-old John Davies had enlisted in August 1914 in the 10th Cheshires at the first call to arms. Unlike so many of his mates, however, he had then developed the longest 'charge sheet' of all of the Lostock contingent. One of three children, John had worked for the Union Acid Company on Manchester Road as an Iron Hamper Maker. He was a popular character about the village, playing football for the local team and bowling for the Lostock Alkali team.

Left to right: Pte.J.T.Faulkner, Pte.A.Macdonald, Crp.H.Postles, Lt-Crp.W.J.Ainsworth

John's disciplinary problems started soon after the 10th Cheshires arrived in France. His record shows that on the 8th December 1915 he was 'awarded 14 days F.P. [Field Punishment] No. 1 for falling out without permission whilst on the march.' Within two weeks of completing that punishment he was back before his brigade commander and 'awarded 21 days F.P. No. 1 for insolence to an N.C.O.'

(Field Punishment No 1 resulted in the prisoner being tied, by ropes or chains, to a fixed object, perhaps a fencepost or a gun wheel, for up to 2 hours in each 24 and for not more than 21 days' duration.)

A mixture of the trench fighting and set battles of 1916, during one of which he received a gunshot wound to his hand and, in the fighting on the Somme in September, a dose of German gas, appears to have calmed John's fiery temper. That is until, in the spring of 1917, his problems restarted when he took unofficial leave for a week, which cost him eight days' pay. Between February 1917 and October 1918, John was charged on at least ten occasions with a variety of offences ranging from using foul and abusive language to an N.C.O to going absent without leave. By the time of his formal demobilization in 1919 the military and John shared a mutual dislike!

Brook Street

No. 3: Martha Gathercole felt that, whilst the old adage 'do it now or never' certainly did not apply in her romantic business with Billy Ainsworth, 'do it now or not for some time' might prove more appropriate. Billy was just two weeks short of his twentieth birthday, in September 1915, when he and Martha, on the last night of his embarkation leave, said their goodbyes. She had been saving for months from her meagre wage as a domestic servant until, at last, she had sufficient to purchase a gold ring, specially monogrammed for her beloved Billy. This simple, hard-earned gift made Billy a man apart. His life, to that moment, had mirrored that of most of his Lostock peers in the

Ruins in Ypres.

early years of the 20th century. After leaving the local boys' school he had worked as a rivet heater at Brunners and was soon enjoying the pleasures of the Lostock Alkali Bowling Team and the Saturday dances in Northwich where he had first met Martha.

The rush to the recruiting office, in August 1914, by the Brunner boys, had Billy at its head. He enlisted, as had so many of his Lostock mates, in the 10th Cheshires and was assigned to 'B' Company. In basic training he stood out and was soon wearing his Lance Corporal's stripe. On arrival in France, as part of the New Armies heading towards the 'Big Push' on the Somme. Billy and his pals arrived in the front line trenches near Ypres in mid-April 1915. He wrote his last letter home on 12th May:

> Dear Mum,
> We are out of the trenches after twenty and a half days. We have had a lot of casualties this time. The scrapping here is pretty lively at times but we have put the wind up the Huns a bit. The other day I had the pleasure of seeing three Huns taken prisoner by our fellows, in fact they came over and gave themselves up. They are fine fellows and were well groomed. I don't think they were short of food as you see it in the papers. They may go short but I candidly tell you, they looked well. Keep on smiling 'till I come home.
> Your son, Billy

'B' Company returned to the front line on 17th May and spent six days in hand-to-hand fighting between bouts of artillery bombardment.

The Battalion War Diary records:

> 20th May 1916   Continuous shelling during morning and afternoon of our communication trenches and resistance line. Two Company H.Q.'s were hit, one being set on fire.

The dreaded telegram arrived at Number 3 on 25th May, followed by a letter from Billy's Company Commander, Lt. J.A.Simmons P:

> Dear Mrs Ainsworth,
> I very much regret to have to inform you that your son L/Cpl. Ainsworth was killed on Saturday by a shell, death being instantaneous.
> He was a very good soldier and we shall miss him very much, but all of us remember that he was one who saw the path of duty and followed it regardless of all costs. All honour to him.
> May I offer you my deepest sympathy in your bereavement.

Enclosed with the letter was a gold ring with the monogram 'W.J.A.' Billy's remains are buried at Ecoivres Military Cemetery, near Mont St. Éloi, whilst his life is commemorated on the family tombstone in St. John's churchyard at Lostock Gralam.

No. 5: A member of the Northwich Adelaide Band, the Witton Brotherhood and the Lostock Alkali Bowling Team, Christopher Johnson had joined the East Lancs. because of their advertisement for drummers, but the Somme reduced his efficiency to nil and, after a period in a Scottish Military hospital suffering from severe shell shock, he was invalided out of the war in early 1917.

No. 12: The Bates brothers, Ben and Harry, both attested within days of the outbreak, Ben joining the 8th Battalion and Harry the 10th Battalion of the Cheshires.

Ben's Service Records in his time in Mesopotamia, reveal a long, long history of tropical diseases and frequent visits to the Casualty Clearing Stations and Field Hospitals. Eventually he was declared to be no longer physically fit to serve and, in December 1916, he was given a pension of 6/3d. for three months, reducing to 3/6d. for the following 91 weeks, to be followed by a review. Harry had fought on the Somme with the 10th Cheshires but, in November 1916, had transferred to the 12th Battalion, who were occupying the relatively 'quiet' zone on the Struma plain. However, in September 1918, a major attack was launched against Pip Ridge, near Doiran.

The enemy counter-attacked in large numbers and inflicted severe casualties. The 12th Battalion almost ceased to exist with under 70 men answering the roll call that night. Amongst the casualties was Harry, who had bullet wounds to both his chest and arm and a damaged pleura. His war was over and, after visits to various Field Hospitals, he was finally transferred to a General Hospital in Malta, significantly on 11th November 1918.

No. 16: Arguably the most tragic of all of the Lostock families, the Connollys, lived at Number 16. Their story has been told earlier.

Victoria Street

Plumber John Smith, his wife, Mary, and their six children had moved into the village from Widnes in the final years of the century. James, their eldest child, had found both work and accommodation on a local farm where he was to live until the war clouds of 1914 started to gather. As a farmhand, James had been in a reserved occupation and for some time enjoyed the benefits of home life with his young wife, Mary. However, as the situation deteriorated in France, James was convinced that he should do his bit and, in 1915, followed his younger brother... into the military, being assigned to the 9th Battalion of the Welsh Regiment.

No service record would appear to exist for James and even his 'medals card' appears to be quite new and supplies little information other than his basic awards. Records show, however, that he was severely wounded in the carnage known as the Battle of Polygon Wood, which involved men from the British, Australian and New Zealand armies. James was rushed to a Casualty Clearing Station but died of his wounds on the 3rd October 1917. He remains in the Communal Cemetery at Outtersteene near Baillent.

The Terriers

JOHN DEAKIN

A NUMBER of young Lostockians had enlisted as 'Terriers' or 'Saturday Night Soldiers' when the Territorial Army was instituted under War Minister Haldane's reforms of 1907. These were young men who enjoyed the challenge of weekly parades and weekend camps in the 5th Battalion of the Cheshire Regiment without having to enlist in the regular army.

Henry Postles of Boundary Street (whose short military life and death are reported elsewhere) had been close friends with John Deakin of Hewitt Street at school, at Brunners and in the community. In 1911 their decision was mutual and they enlisted – their given army numbers (Henry 1521 and John 1524) recording their closeness. They embarked for France with their unit in February 1915. Within six weeks Henry was killed outside Ypres; John's war was only just beginning. His battalion was deemed to be of the best quality and their Brigadier issued the following order:

A section of 'The Terriers', 1/5th Cheshires.

> In saying farewell to the 5th Battalion, which is leaving the 14th Brigade and being formed into a Pioneer Battalion, [I] place on record [my] very high appreciation [of them]. The conduct of the 5th Cheshires, both in the field and in billets, has been exemplary, and the fact that they have been selected for formation into a Pioneer Battalion is proof of the excellence of their work.

As Pioneers, the 1/5 Cheshires would be expected, essentially, to perform two roles – as engineers working on repairing the often shattered lines of communication (roads, trenches, bridges, tracks etc.) and, in times of urgency, as front-line fighting men. John and his comrades, part of the newly-formed 56th (London) Division since February 1916, were preparing for that great bloodshed, which was to win lasting notoriety as the Battle of the Somme. They were to be part of the attack on Gommecourt at the northern end of the July 1st British front line, the village having been targeted as the site of a 'diversionary' action where it was hoped that the increased preparations during June 1916 would divert the Germans' attention from the main attack line. The 'diversion' failed. Even though the enemy concentrated vast quantities of heavy armament on the area, it did little to turn the Germans' attention away from the so-called main line of attack, stretching between the villages of Serre and Montaubon. On that first terrible day, July 1st 1916, the 1/5 were the only Cheshires to go 'over the top'. By evening roll call, some 300 of the Battalion, over 700 strong at morning stand-to, were casualties. John Deakin was a survivor. However, his death was merely on hold. On 10th August his family back in Lostock received the news that John was in a military hospital having been seriously wounded by heavy German shell fire whilst his Company was repairing damaged roads a mere three miles from the Gommecourt salient.

John lingered for three weeks in the Main Dressing Station at Bronfay Farm, but, on the 8th September 1916 he lost his final battle. He is buried in the Bronfay Farm Military Cemetery at Bray-sur-Somme.

EDWARD ASHLEY

Living within one hundred yards of both the Hewitt and Postles families were the Ashleys. Edward and Mary had brought their family of five children from Runcorn to the greener pastures of Lostock in 1898. Work was guaranteed at Brunner's whilst there was good accommodation available along Manchester Road.

Pte.E. Ashley

Edward had settled in the Lostock schools and had followed, in 1907, the trail to Brunner's established by his dad and elder brothers. However, seduced no doubt by the promise of a short but exciting trip to France, Edward joined the Cheshire Regiment in early 1915 and, on the 26th September, crossed to France as a recruit for the 1/5th Cheshires, now serving as a Pioneer Battalion to the newly-formed 56th Division, preparing for the 'Big Push' on the Somme. Despite his Battalion being consistently under heavy fire in the battles at Morval and Le Transloy, Edward survived as the Somme bloodshed slithered to its conclusion in the cloying mud of November.

It is possible that the 1/5th Cheshires spent at least part of the winter of 1917 helping with the development of the tunnels and caves under the town of Arras. Certainly they assembled there in preparation for the attacks along the Scarpe River, which began on the 9th April. Sadly, Edward did not report for roll call after the severe shelling endured by his Battalion whilst repairing the trenches along the Arras-Cambrai road on the night of 8th May 1917. As his remains were never found Edward is commemorated, along with over 35,000 other Commonwealth soldiers from the sector who have no known grave, on the Arras Memorial.

The Pickerings of Manchester Road

BY THE summer of 1914, the Pickerings found themselves in that social group identified as both well-established in the community and comfortable in their environment. William and Jane had lived in Lostock since their marriage and, during the ensuing thirty years 119 Manchester Road had become home to their five sons and two daughters. William had started life in the village of Davenham but, on leaving school, had moved with his recently-widowed mum to Lostock Gralam where he had found employment in the Wincham Corn and Bone Mill on Manchester Road. In 1884 he had married and, determined to look after the two women in his life, his mum and new wife Jane, he had rented a house just doors away from the former. After a devout Wesleyan upbringing, William ensured that each of his seven children, born between 1886 and 1898, were carefully schooled in the teachings of the faith. So regular was the family's attendance at the Wesleyan Church on Manchester Road that, by 1905, William had graduated from the simple duties of Sunday School teacher to being School Superintendent. Furthermore, his dedication at the Bone Mill had seen him promoted to Mill Engine Driver, a job much more prestigious and far better paid than that of ordinary labourer. Jane enjoyed life. She was liked and respected in the village; her children brought her nothing but credit and her husband was widely admired. Financially, the family were in a good position, especially when the boys started work. William had planned carefully for his sons. Not for them the back-breaking labour in the mills – rather should they thrive in white-collar jobs and in 1900 Joseph established a family tradition when he left school and began work as a trainee booking clerk at Northwich Railway Station. Within two years brother John was to follow suit and, in 1906, William became the third railway clerk in the Pickering family.

Young Henry was to break the sequence. He had always enjoyed dashing round after school to Mr Robert's grocery shop in Station Road to keep the yard tidy and make any deliveries. Thus, when he left school in 1908, he was pleased to be offered a full-time job in the shop. However, whilst he liked both his work and his employer, Henry was normally penniless by mid-week and, in 1912, with Mr Robert's reluctant support, he secured a better paid job as a shipping clerk at the Brunner Mond works. By the summer of 1913, the Pickering family were secretly envied by some of the Lostock residents. Both daughters were employed in the 'better' Northwich shops; all of the boys were fashioning good careers for themselves and William Senior had recently been appointed to Foreman Engine Driver.

The good news continued; Sam, the youngest of the boys, had managed, possibly with Dad's help, to gain an apprenticeship with Mr Parker as a joiner; and Christmas 1913 was worthy of extra celebration with the news that William Junior was to be promoted to Senior Booking Clerk and moved to Central Railway Station in the heart of Manchester.

However, within twelve months the sense of well-being at 119 Manchester Road was put under serious threat by the Outbreak. Just like the Connolly brothers of Brook Street, William and Henry were given consecutive army numbers when they enlisted together on 3rd September 1914 in the 11th Battalion of the Cheshire Regiment. Jane was concerned, but at least her sons would be able to look after each other and their years of service in the local St. John's Ambulance Brigade, under their Dad's supervision, could prove most useful if they ran into difficulties. Whatever might happen, Christmas was not far off and everybody was sure that the war would not extend into 1915.

The Pickering boys left for training at Codford St. Mary, near Salisbury, in late September. Conditions were so bad *(History of the Cheshire Regiment in the Great War – Col. Arthur Crookenden, Page 344)* in their mud-strewn camp that mutiny was threatened. Lieutenant C.F. Hill, a footballer of international standing, prevented disaster by issuing an extra ration of beer and promising to bring the men's grievances to the Commanding Officer, Colonel Dyas's, attention. Dyas was already in touch with Lord Kitchener who, aware that a nearby battalion had already deserted en masse, ordered an immediate move to comfortable billets near Bournemouth and leave to be granted in strict rotation with immediate effect. Hence Henry and William detrained in the familiar surroundings of Northwich Station on Christmas Eve 1914 in time to join the congregation at their Manchester Road church for the Christmas celebrations. Throughout the spring and summer of 1915, with their battalion involved in divisional manoeuvres at their new camp near Winchester, the boys were granted a couple more home leaves until, in early autumn, they were able to tell the family that an overseas 'trip' was imminent.

The Lost Boys of Lostock

Jane's concerns were not without foundation. News was thick on the ground of the large numbers of Lostock boys who were being sacrificed on the battlefields of Northern Europe. As usual, her husband's normal mantra, 'God will provide', gave her strength.

On the 27th September 1915 the two brothers, along with the rest of the 11th Cheshires, landed at Le Havre. The French 'adventure' was about to begin!

There was to be no settling-in period. A fierce British attack to drive the Germans from their position on a line from the La Bassée Canal to the town of Loos, one of several ill-conceived battle-plans of this war, had led to very heavy British casualties. As Crookenden reports:

> Often orders were issued by Divisional H.Q. for a position to be captured which had already been won and, at such heavy sacrifice, that it had been lost again before the orders arrived!

Once the battle reached its inevitable stalemate, the 11th Cheshires were ordered to defend the trenches in a line near Ploegstreet Wood, where they were to remain intermittently until the spring of 1916.

In May of that year the Germans, completely fazed by the mining activity under their various strongholds on the Ridge itself, launched an attack on the British trenches just below Vimy. Hand-to-hand fighting and the use of hundreds of hand-thrown bombs had wreaked havoc among the defending forces, resulting in many casualties. The brothers, however, survived and, no doubt because of the large number of non-commissioned officer casualties, both won immediate promotions to full Sergeant, news which gave Jane, back in Lostock, some temporary relief from her almost permanent state of foreboding.

The last letter from the boys, in early June, hinted at some 'big plan' being laid which would surely bring the war to a swift end. The 'big plan' was, in fact, to find realisation on the 1st July when over one hundred thousand, mainly young, Englishmen, left their trenches and walked across no-man's-land to signal the beginning of the Battle of the Somme.

On the big day the Cheshires had been held in reserve until, on the 2nd, they had been ordered to Martinsart from where, on the 3rd, they launched an attack in the vicinity of Thiepval. Again the battalion was engaged in heavy and, sadly, badly-planned fighting. Little had been gained near Thiepval on July 1st and the 11th Cheshires were to suffer numerous casualties defending these 'scraps'. Amongst them was William Pickering. A shell had exploded alongside his position, causing severe wounds to his arm and shoulder. He had been rushed to the Field Ambulance and from there to a military hospital in Boulogne. As even more specialist treatment was required William was hurriedly shipped to the Kent and Canterbury Hospital from where, on the 7th July, a postcard had been sent informing the family of his plight but not its seriousness. No news had been received from Henry, and Jane worried, simply worried. Despite the assurances of her sons and daughters, that same sense of foreboding, which had gripped her as the boys ended their embarkation leaves, was now troubling her more than ever. Her bag-packing in preparation for a dash to visit William in hospital was halted by the postman's knock and, subsequently, the sound of sobbing as Jane received the tell-tale telegram. William had died of complications to his dreadful wounds on the morning of the 16th July. Within days more mail was to arrive, firstly from Henry, querying his brother's welfare. He had last seen him being stretchered away and had heard of his repatriation; since then, nothing. Later that week, letters were to arrive from William's C.O. and the padre to the 11th Cheshires. There were only first class reports on the late Sergeant William Pickering: popular with his men, conscientious and thoroughly dependable. Jane knew all of that – but he was gone!

Mr J.A. Cowley, Hon. Secretary to the Northwich Fund, came to ask if he could be of any help and was only too willing to assist when she confided that she would like her son brought home. Within days, Cowley had received a telegram, agreeing to his request, from the military authorities. Jane would have preferred a simple family interment but the propaganda value of the district seeing one of its own laid to rest, with full military ceremony, was not to be missed. William Senior persuaded his wife that this was as it should be and so, on the morning of the 21st July 1916, the funeral cortège left the family home en route for the nonconformist section of the Northwich Churchyard. Lostock Gralam stopped as the coffin, on a wheeled bier covered with a Union Jack, on which rested William's helmet, belt and bayonet, and led by the bugles and men of the King's Shropshire Light Infantry, processed down Manchester Road. Marching behind came a number of William's old pals, who were either recuperating or home on leave. Amongst their number were George Goulding, George Marlow, Joe Garner, Henry Illidge and Charlie Stubbs. Within three short years each of them would have made the supreme sacrifice. The family and friends followed in four coaches. William's fiancée, Lily Coombs, was inconsolable. They had been engaged since the night of William's enlistment in September 1914 but had agreed to wait a few months until the 'madness' had finished before tying the knot. Now, two years later, the war continued in full fury whilst William had found permanent peace. Dozens of the young people from the Sunday School classes which William had taught, waited at the churchyard. There were hundreds of friends of the family who had known William from childhood, since the days when he had delivered their heavy orders from Bob Robert's grocery. The mourners overflowed the church to hear the Reverend Calvert perform the last rites and, to the sound of a three-volley salute and the playing of the Last Post, Sergeant William Pickering was laid to his final rest. Significantly, buried in a family grave with Joseph, his grandfather and William his dad who died in 1938, William lies without the comfort of a C.W.G.C. headstone. In France, Henry marked the hour of his brother's committal in silent prayer. He had asked for furlough to attend the funeral but the Battle of the Somme was at its height and, as a newly-promoted Sergeant himself, he was too valuable to his battalion to be spared for a funeral, an event which had somehow lost its old significance being a daily, multiple occurrence in the France of 1916.

One face of the Lostock Gralam memorial.

Despite the family concern when eighteen-year-old Sam announced, early in the new year, that he had joined the Cheshires, 1917 brought some joy into the Pickering household. John, the second son, had married Grace McLean from nearby Tabley in late spring. Best man was young Sam, on special leave, resplendent in his new uniform.

In July there was another wedding to celebrate. Henry had been sent home from the Front to begin Officer Training on the recommendation of his Commanding Officer. The shortage of subalterns after the battles of the previous twelve months had become pressing and Henry Pickering was prime material. Knowing what might await him on his return to France where his first platoon awaited, Henry had been delighted when his girlfriend of some four years standing, Elsie, had accepted his proposal of marriage. The last big family occasion was also by way of being a farewell party for Henry who, on 27th September, had been granted a Second Lieutenancy in the South Lancashire Regiment.

The first news of the second family tragedy reached Manchester Road during the second week of March 1918. The South Lancs. had been engaged in defending the line near Givenchy against a series of fierce German attacks. Henry had led his platoon's resistance valiantly but had been seriously wounded, along with a number of his men, by shell-fire. Despite the best efforts of the Field Ambulance, Henry had succumbed to his wounds on the 9th March.

2nd-Lt. H.E Pickering

Gorre British and Indian Cemetery, near the town of Bethune on Festubert Road, is in the grounds of the old Gorre Château. Henry lies alongside a half dozen of his men, killed in the same fighting and, possibly, by the same shell. His stone lies near the Great Cross, in the shade of a huge hedge, along with a large number of men from the 55th (West Lancs.) Division. A memorial service was held for Henry in St. John's in late April attended by the grieving family and Elsie on one of her last visits to Lostock Gralam. She returned to her family home in Dundee, mourned her young husband for some three years and, eventually, having remarried, moved to a new life in Alberta, Canada.

English Artillery heading for the Front in 1914.

The Lost Boys of Lostock

The Southern Boys

GEORGE Southern's heart lay in farming. He had thoroughly enjoyed life in his home village of Mere, Cheshire, working John Wilkinson's one hundred acres. However, after his marriage to Sarah in 1884 and with the arrival of their first born imminent, George knew that he needed a house and a better income for his small family. The Northwich Brick Works offered both and Sarah was delighted. Now she would be able to create their first home, close to her birthplace in Lostock Gralam and with the open spaces her young husband loved within a few hundred yards. Number 8 School Lane was an unprepossessing terraced house but it was quickly to become Sarah's nest. Whilst George set off for work down the old Roman road, she used her day to beg items of furniture from her family and to make the two mile walk to Northwich market to buy inexpensive remnants of material which would become covers and curtains for Number 8.

Their first born, Thomas, arrived in December 1884, to be joined almost two years to the day later by William. From then on and at approximately two year intervals, Sarah delivered male babies – George junior in April 1889, John in February 1893, Charles in April 1896 and, finally, Henry (affectionately known as Harry) in 1898. Despite the hardships of rearing six boys on a labourer's wages, Sarah enjoyed life on School Lane. The neighbours were friendly, large families common and George senior delighted in his Sunday stroll down Station Road, through the Hollows, and into the hamlet of Lostock Green, where the Cheshire countryside began in earnest. Sunday lunch always followed the Matins at St. John's, where, in turn, the Southern boys had been baptised. Sarah hardly ever missed the Sunday morning observances at church, accompanied by her ever-increasing flock. The six brothers each attended the local school between 1890, when Tom was admitted, and 1913, when Henry, the last in line, closed that chapter on the family history.

By 1898, George senior had returned to his first love, working on the land and, on leaving school, Tom had managed to find work and accommodation on Hulse Farm at Allostock, which meant that he could spend Sundays in School Lane after a three mile walk across the fields. The outdoor life suited Tom, and young William emulated his brother in 1900.

The Lost Boys of Lostock

The younger boys enjoyed the extra space in the shared bedroom but missed their big brothers nevertheless. However, their peace was short lived. Tom was missing the team practices with Lostock Gralam Football Club and William was not seeing enough of Ellen Bramhall from nearby Fitton Street, his 'fancy' since leaving school. Within a mere couple of years, No. 8 was back to its usual capacity, but there had been a price to pay for the two eldest brothers – their country life was done and Brunner Mond now had two more employees.

Finances at No. 8 were now easing and George junior would contribute to the pot in 1905 when he secured a job as a trainee engine washer, working for the Great Central Railway at Northwich Steam Sheds. He spoke so enthusiastically about his work that 14-year-old John was pleased to join him there in 1907. The single biggest event in the family history occurred when William and Ellen married at St. John's on May Day in 1909. Sarah could barely conceal her delight as her five sons stood witness to their brother's vows. She had her concerns about the future, especially where the health of her husband was concerned. George senior had determined to improve the family's lot by taking the solid wage and regular overtime available at Brunner Mond but the wracking cough he had endured years before at the Brickworks had returned. Yet an even greater threat to the Southern family's happiness loomed. With her fifth son, Charles, established at Brunner Mond along with his dad and two eldest brothers, Sarah was able to concentrate on little Harry's future. The family was well respected in the area and George senior often broke his Sunday walk to chat to his cousin George, Station Master at Lostock Gralam. In 1912, as his youngest son left school, George senior, urged by Sarah, asked his cousin to recommend Harry for the trainee porter's post which had become available. Thus, by the spring of 1914, the Southern family was well set. Sarah's concerns about George senior's dreadful cough cost her many nights' sleep, but at least her six boys appeared to be well established. Tom was a minor celebrity in the village, both on the football field and on the village bowling green; William and Ellen had settled into pleasant domesticity; George junior and John enjoyed the fishing with their dad over Wincham Flashes; Charles was keen on sport – and also on the new girl, Belinda, whose family had recently moved into Number 31; finally Harry was doing so well at the station that his Uncle George forecast great things for him.

In early August 1914, the excitement at Brunner Mond was tangible. War had been declared and great opportunities for a view of the world outside North Cheshire now existed for young men, but speed was of the essence as informed opinion predicted that all would be over by Christmas. Tom needed no urging. He knew of the sporting facilities in the Army, he had always defended his brothers from bullies and what else was Germany but a bloated aggressor? Tea time, Friday 21st August, life at No. 8 School Lane began its metamorphosis. Tom announced that he had come directly from the recruiting office and was now an enlisted man in the 2nd Battalion of the Rifle Brigade. Sarah was numb. What did it mean? Her husband, George, was a sick man and her eldest son would soon be off to . . . where?

Little time remained for either trepidation or recrimination. The Brigade had just completed nearly two years on garrison duty in India and were looking forward to some extended leave in 'Blighty'. However events in the Balkans caused major realignment of their orders. They docked in Liverpool on 22nd October 1914 from whence, after a respite lasting no more than a few days to allow them to re-equip, to re-armour and to reinforce, they sailed again, this time for France, with Tom a proud member of their number.

The Brigade's first serious action was at the Battle of Amber Ridge when, as part of the 8th Division, they attacked in the first wave across a No Man's Land of no more than 150 yards at 5.30am on 9th May 1915. A bloody fight ensued and despite the Rifles giving a good account of themselves, they suffered enormous casualties from the German machine guns. At the roll call that evening, of the 830 men who had jumped off that morning, only 180 answered to their names.

Tom Southern was not there. He had last been seen lying severely wounded but within the perimeter of the German wire. News filtered in that he had been seen being carried back behind the German lines to an uncertain future. In the confusion of those spring days of 1915, the news reaching Number 8 School Lane was simply that Rifleman Thomas Southern was 'missing; believed captured' and even though Sarah feared the worst, at best her eldest might still be alive. Throughout the period of waiting, the family was in turmoil. With the sole exception of the youngest, Harry, all of Sarah's boys had enlisted within weeks of the Outbreak and the comings and goings at School Lane seemed never-ending. William, along with his cousin and best friend, Harry Fellows of Winnington, had joined the East Lancashire Regiment, despite the protests of Ellen that there were still large numbers of single men who had not enlisted; but the departure to the colours of unmarried younger brothers, George and Charles, somehow settled the argument. The 8th Battalion of the Cheshire Regiment was soon to count Charles amongst its complement, while George, along with many of his pals, had joined the

Cheshire Regiment and been assigned to the 10th Battalion, made up largely of local boys. Indeed, this unit, more than any other, was to surrender a greater number of Lostock men to the military cemeteries of the Great War.

Twenty-one-year-old John had accompanied Charles and George to the recruiting office and, after a few days' consideration, he too accepted the King's shilling and joined the same regiment. The consequences, when Sarah heard the news, were quite imaginable. She left John in no doubt that he should have stayed at home with young Harry, especially as their father was so ill and unable to do a full week's work at Brunner's without needing a couple of days to recover.

However, the deeds were done. Number 8 School Lane, normally a world of drying laundry, lost socks, hob-nailed boots and Saturday-night clean shirts, was now virtually empty. Sixteen-year-old Harry was enjoying work as a trainee porter at the local railway station and was showing no interest in following his brothers, but Sarah could not relax.

There was still no news of Tom; Charles had been quickly despatched to somewhere called the Dardanelles; whilst the other three boys had all sailed for France, after brief embarkation leaves full of hope and patriotic talk. Ellen, William's wife, shared Sarah's concern especially as news of the sacrificed boys of the district started to appear in the local paper. Indeed Sammy Whittaker, who had been missing since the great battle of August 1914, was frequently featured in the press; and now Tom was in the platoon of the missing. In September 1915, devastation! A telegram arrived from the War Office with the almost expected news – Rifleman Thomas Southern had died in an enemy field hospital on 13th May. Sarah's heart all but stopped. Not only had she lost her eldest son but she had to tell his dad, currently in the sick bed he had occupied for some two months. George senior merely stared into space as Sarah read the telegram to him. Never again would they share a Friday evening pint at the 'Slow and Easy' or take their customary Sunday stroll through Lostock Hollows. A light had gone out in her husband's life and Sarah could only watch and fret. Within one week, George senior was dead. The doctor said it was lung disease but Sarah knew it was more.

Bad news followed bad. John had not written for nearly a month before a field postcard arrived to say he had been taken prisoner and was now in Rennbahn, Germany.

William wrote whenever his duties allowed. He appeared to be well but rarely mentioned the fighting. In October 1915 the compassionate side of William's nature permeates his letter to his Aunt in Winnington:

The Lost Boys of Lostock

Dear Aunt Elsie,

The task I have set myself of writing to you is extremely difficult because it is as painful to me as it will be to you. It is with the utmost regret that I take the duty of telling you that dear Harry was killed in action with many other brave fellows. It happened that a shell burst in the dug out where Harry and several of his comrades were situated and I am sorry to say that Harry was killed while the others were badly injured. His death was instantaneous and he suffered no pain as I myself saw him soon after and he was beyond all human aid.

I hardly know what to say to alleviate somewhat the stroke that has fallen so heavily upon you and many others but you may rest assured he died a brave soldier and a man. The blow is heavy but may God comfort you in your great distress. None of us know whether it will be our turn next so we feel it keenly when one is taken away from us. Be brave, Aunt, and someday again the sun will shine and peace will reign.

'All the lads offer their deepest sympathy to you in your great loss and trust that a speedy peace may soon be obtained. Harry will be given a Christian burial in a British cemetery behind the lines and as soon as I can ascertain where he is buried I will write again. I am very thankful I am well. They were all Northwich lads who were hurt by the shell which killed Harry. I never had such a shock as when I saw him.

Your loving nephew, William

Sarah longed for 1916 to begin. The old year had brought her nothing but grief with the loss of her husband, her first-born and a much loved nephew, her sister's boy.

In early January she received news that Charles was coming home for good from the Dardanelles. Stricken down by the Turkish guns, he had been evacuated by hospital ship from Savla Bay and was to take no further part in the war. His welcome at Number 8 was necessarily subdued, but offered a part answer to Sarah's prayers. If young Harry, now 17 years old, had harboured doubts about staying at home, these doubts were quickly removed by Charles's stories of life in the war zone known as Gallipoli. He ensured that his young brother was spared none of the horrors and, as if in final confirmation, a letter arrived at the Southern household on Monday 24th July 1916, sent from a Field Post Office in France.

Rifleman T.Southern (left)
Pte.G.Southern

The Lost Boys of Lostock

Dear Mrs. Southern,
 I deeply regret to inform you that your son, Private George Southern, was killed in action four days ago whilst endeavouring to rescue a wounded comrade during a fierce attack on the enemy's line. It was an action typical of your son to whom all of the officers and men of the Battalion would wish to pay tribute to his heroism.
He was a first class soldier who never shirked his duty and always bore himself with dignity.
Please accept the sincere condolences for you and your family from every man in the 10th Cheshires.

Yours sincerely,
2nd Lt. J.V.Wilson

In the two-day Battle of Bazentin during which George had fallen, the Battalion suffered nearly four hundred casualties, for a net gain of no land. A steady stream of visitors came to Number 8 to voice their sympathies, not least from the Great Central Railway Steam Sheds in Northwich where the late George had worked in the eleven years between his leaving school and his enlistment. In late August, Sarah and Ellen were sitting in the rear garden while Harry and Charles were watching the bowling at the 'Slow and Easy', when the latch clicked. Sarah expected to see Edith Hulme from up the lane who had become a regular visitor since her husband, too, had been killed the month previously, probably in the same battle as George. Sarah's heart skipped a beat. Standing there was John, weary looking and definitely a stone lighter, but still her boy, John. Along with a group of friends, he had managed to escape from the German camp at Rennbahn, helped by the fact that the compound had been established on a racecourse and was hopelessly overcrowded with some 12,000 prisoners. They had slipped away through an unguarded drainage system, made their way to the Dutch border and, from there, back to the British lines. John now had a long leave to recuperate, not only from his trials in Rennbahn, but also from the news, tearfully given to him by his mother, of the deaths of his dad and George. John tackled his demons in the 'Slow and Easy' and other various hostelries in Northwich. In October, after spending much of the day in the company of a group of other disabled and released ex-soldiers, deploring the fact that there were still 'Huns' living in the town, they turned their drunken wrath on the premises of C. Fisher, Witton Street, Northwich, fuelled by the rumour that his name was really spelt 'Fischer'. The shop lost its plate glass window, valued at £11.00 and John appeared before the magistrates on 9th October, still clutching a bottle of whisky. Because he had a date in London with the 'Returned P. O.W.s' Society' to report on his treatment at the hands of the Germans, John was granted bail in a £10.00 bond and his whisky withheld until his return to court.

By now, Harry, traumatised by the succession of emotional hammer blows that had struck the family and especially his mother, had received his call to arms. Sarah would not hear of it. Had her family not endured enough? She appeared throughout 1917 at a succession of Military Tribunals pleading for exemption for her youngest. The best she could achieve were six monthly deferments until March 1918. As the presiding officer put it, 'This family has contributed five sons to the Colours, of whom two are dead, one disabled, one an ex-prisoner and the fifth still fighting. Lately the husband has died, adding to their burden. The case is made. The sixth son shall be granted the maximum exemption of six months until 30th September 1918.

Harry never went to war. Charles, too, was done with battle. William came home after the Armistice and settled into a peaceful existence with Ellen, working on various farms. Little is on record of how John spent the remainder of his life but there is no record of him ever having married. As for the 'lost' brothers – Thomas is buried in Laventie Military Cemetery, near the town of La Gorgue in the Nord Region of France having been moved there after the war from the German cemetery at Roubaix; George's body was given a battlefield burial but his grave was permanently lost, probably destroyed by shell fire in an ensuing conflict. His name is remembered in perpetuity, along with those of over 73,000 other casualties of the Somme battles who have no known grave, on the mighty Thiepval memorial.

The regeneration of the Southerns began five years after the war's end, in May 1923, when, to Sarah's great delight, Charles married Belinda Riley. There, were significantly, three empty chairs at the wedding breakfast in the function room at the 'Slow and Easy', but Sarah felt that there was, at last, something of a future to look forward to.

The Foxleys of Station Road

AS THE nineteenth century drew to a close, John Foxley decided that the time was ripe to take over the Smithy, just off Manchester Road, in Lostock Gralam. Bertha, his wife, appreciating the opportunity that such a move would present and knowing that a neat little house, just around the corner from John's forge, was available to rent, prepared to leave their home in nearby Marston. Ten-year-old William was less enthusiastic. Life in Marston village was familiar. He liked his school and was a well-integrated member of the community, but Bertha stifled all his protests. There was no choice. A good job awaited his dad and, anyway, Lostock was not so far from Marston that he would never see his mates again. Besides, he must set a big brother's example to eight year old Joseph, who was even more fearful of the move. In early June 1898, the family left the security of Marston for the short journey to Lostock Gralam. Only one year old Albert was totally unconcerned. He was much more interested in the ride on the cart carrying the family's chattels through the Cheshire lanes. Number Two Station Road was ideal for the small family. With two bedrooms and a useful yard, it was at the centre of the village. A goodly number of local shops were within yards, the church and school were both within walking distance and John would appreciate the two popular licensed houses on adjacent corners just across the Manchester Road.

Apart from the normal concerns of a mother setting up a new home for her family, Bertha's main concern lay at the top of Station Road where it joined Manchester Road – locally to become known either as Prosecution Corner or, more commonly, Conviction Crossroads. This was the main route from Manchester to Chester, and consequently, the still-new 'horseless carriages' could be speed tested by enthusiastic young bloods heading down the long, straight stretch leading to and from Northwich. However Bertha was calmed when John pointed out that he would be the one risking the vehicles when he took his nightly pint at either 'The Slow and Easy' or 'The Black Greyhound'. William's big day arrived on 20th June 1898 when, accompanied by young Joe, Mum took him to the Boys' School where, admission register duly completed, the boys joined their new classmates and quietly learned that the Snelsons, the Mathers and the Goodiers, from nearby Lostock Green, were well-known characters, both in the school and in the district.

The Foxleys flourished in Lostock. John earned a good income in Smithy Lane and William was able to contribute to the family's finances when he joined the daily migration to Lostock Works in 1901. Bertha made her contribution to the family, too, when she presented John with a baby daughter. The boys were also delighted, even little Albert, now firmly established in the Infants' School. He enjoyed his new-found status as a 'big' brother and, given the task of telling the neighbourhood in Station Road of the new arrival, he was really pleased to be given a celebratory gob-stopper by Mrs. Roberts at the grocer's shop. On leaving school in 1904, Joe followed William to Brunner Mond Salt Works but, unlike him, managed to secure employment in the laboratories of the company, based in Winnington. Young Albert continued to make progress at school and such was his leaving report that he managed to break the family work-cycle – a work-cycle pursued by the greater majority of Lostock men – and obtained a job as an apprentice tailor, working for George Thompson, a reputable firm, with branches in Northwich and St. Anne's-on-Sea. His diligence quickly won the admiration of his employer who gave him an enhanced training position at the St. Anne's branch in 1915 – a vacancy having been created by the departure of a Thompson employee to a training battalion.

On September 1st 1914, Bertha received the news that so many mothers were to share – both William and Joseph had enlisted in the Cheshire Regiment. John was proud and took his boys to 'The Slow and Easy' to reflect on what glories lay ahead. His boys were right to sign up as quickly as possible – after all the war would only last until Christmas and they didn't want to miss all the fun did they? Albert was less than pleased. He was just seventeen – too young to go – and his mother had said that he must finish his training at Thompson's or he might lose the job permanently. Thoughts of going to the recruiting office in Northwich and adding one year to his actual age crossed his mind. Yet, knowing how determined his mother could be, visions of her dragging him out of the marching line by the ear did not sit comfortably with Albert. Sense prevailed. William and Joe were quickly on their way. The 10th Cheshires assembled in Chester during the first week in September and, with neither uniform nor equipment, they were sent with the new battalion to Codford St. Mary near Salisbury in Wiltshire for their initial training. Chaos reigned!

The Lost Boys of Lostock

In sole command of over 800 men for the first two weeks was a quite inexperienced subaltern, Lieutenant E.P. Nares, who did not have even the support of experienced N.C.O.s..

> The next day Lieut. Nares fell in the whole Battalion (or as many of them as he could find) and organized them into Companies and Platoons. He chose provisional N.C.O.s. purely from what they had been doing in civil life, and gave them one, two or three ribbons to tie round their arms. Even this ribbon he had to provide himself. This job took practically the whole day, and there was only time over to give an elementary lecture on camp sanitation, the necessity for which was very obvious after the first night.
> The two following days resembled the break of the monsoon, and as the men had only the clothes they stood up in and one blanket, they had to stay in their tents. A few days later twelve large marine sergeants appeared to the great relief of the Adjutant. Training then started in earnest, principally P.T. and elementary squad drill.
>
> *Crookenden (P.344)*

Christmas 1914 came and went. In Lostock, as throughout the country, the talk was simply of the need for more recruits to deal with the ever-deteriorating situation in France and Belgium. Dreadful losses had been suffered at Mons, where the 1st Cheshires had taken a beating and been forced to retreat in the early weeks of the war. News was filtering back to Lostock that a number of the local boys were, at best, missing or wounded – otherwise something much worse. Joe MacDonald from Boundary Street managed to get a card home to say that he was enjoying German hospitality in the company of Jack Rutledge from nearby Renshaw Street. Harold Deakin of Ann Street had been captured with John Blane from Austin Street in the first real battle of the war and they were now at Paderborn in Germany, but Sammy Whittaker of Griffiths Lane had simply vanished on the 24th August 1914.

In 'The Slow and Easy', 'The Black Greyhound', Wright's Butchers in Station Road and indeed, in all of the regular meeting places, the realization was spreading that this dreadful war was not going to suddenly stop. There was much more heartache to come.

Young Albert Foxley was pressing his case for enlistment more strongly than ever. He was needed – didn't the posters, the sergeants at the recruiting campaigns and even the Reverend Uttley say so in his weekly sermons at St. John's. And his curate, the Reverend Cumber, who had been amongst the first to enlist, had aroused the patriotic feelings of the whole community in his address to the congregation at the Sunday morning service on 23rd May 1915. Harold Cumber was a popular young man who had his lodgings at the vicarage in Station Road and found enjoyment in an occasional game of bowls on the Lostock Alkali green with the workers in the salt industry. He had 'done his duty' by enlisting in October 1914 into the Honorable Artillery Company being sent to France almost immediately. Harold had told an enthralled St. John's of the events of Christmas morning 1914. He had been in a trench no more than eighty yards from the German front line. As the dawn broke, the guns were silent and Harold's attention had been drawn to a huge sheet which had appeared above the German parapet, nailed to two long poles. On it, in bold black letters was written in English:

> We are Saxons. You are Anglo-Saxons.
> If you won't shoot – we won't!
> There are no Prussians here

For that day, at least, a truce was maintained at many points along the front line, but the simple gesture was soon brought to an immediate end, High Command had branded it 'fraternization with the enemy'. Even Harold Cumber had his regrets. He had wished that the banner had stated: 'We are Christians. You are Christians' – but to what purpose one can only imagine. However, Boxing Day had been true to its name – and the savagery had recommenced. Within the month Harold was severely wounded in the cheek and after recuperation in England, ended his war on the staff of a training battalion.

Bertha, clutching her youngest child's hand, had walked quietly home from church. The curate had brought words of hope from the front line, but his message had been rendered less effective by the heavy bandage around his head and the ever-increasing casualty lists in the local paper. Would she be able to continue her resistance to Albert's pleas to join his older brothers in training? Perhaps a divinity intervened, both in George Thompson's tailoring business and at a dance in Lostock Pavilion. A vacancy had occurred at Thompson's St. Anne's branch and Albert fitted the bill. Almost simultaneously he had met Kathleen Harvey from Northwich. Although the move meant promotion and more money, he hated the idea of trusting to the Saturday evening train from Blackpool to Manchester, connecting to the Cheshire Lines to Lostock, where Kathleen would be waiting. At least he could see her every weekend. Late in 1915, William came home for good. As a small boy he had suffered from a bronchial complaint, and now he had been declared unfit for further service. At least he would have no difficulty finding work when he was well.

Joseph prospered in 'B' Company of the 10th Cheshire Battalion. He was popular with his comrades, liked by the N.C.O.s, and his performance as a stretcher bearer and general, all-round platoon man was noted by his officers.

In the spring of 1916 the Battalion was in reserve near Vimy Ridge. Despite the nightly raids and the incessant shelling, the feeling that a big push was being prepared did not occur to Joseph. He wrote home regularly and, on 16th May, wrote to Albert in his lodgings in St. Anne's. He described his life in the trenches, teased him about his fast-developing relationship with Kathleen and ended:

Pte.J.Foxley (left)
Gnr.A.V.Foxley

> The war is still raging and I cannot say how long it will last. It is up to everyone to assist in some way or other and so bring it to a speedy end.

Albert showed the letter to Bertha and John on his next visit home, Saturday 20th May. He had been pricked by his brother's words but Kathleen was proving to be a serious factor. Patriotism or Love? Next day, Albert was almost pleased to catch the afternoon train back to St. Anne's. There, at least, he hoped he would be able to think more lucidly about his problem. Love or Patriotism? The decision was to be wrenched from his hands. On Friday 26th May, Bertha was standing at the front door talking to Sarah Southern from nearby School Lane. The war had brought great sadness to her family and Bertha liked to offer a friendly ear. As the postman turned into Station Road, Bertha felt the first tremors of concern. He came somewhat hesitantly towards the two ladies and handed Bertha an official-looking letter. Almost without realising it, she noticed how his hand trembled slightly. The envelope bore a Field Post Office Cancellation – just as on the letters from Joseph – but the handwriting was not his. Fearing the worst, Bertha withdrew the contents:

> Dear Mrs Foxley,
> It is with the deepest sorrow that I write to you to acquaint you of the death of your son, Private J. Foxley, who was killed by shell fire on Saturday. Death was instantaneous. The only bright feature of the whole affair is that everyone, your son included, did their duty magnificently under very trying circumstances.

The Lost Boys of Lostock

Your son was an extremely good soldier and a fine young man. He will be missed by us all. I had known him since the battalion was formed and on two occasions he was offered sergeant's rank, but he preferred to remain with his friends.
 Please accept my deepest sympathy in your bereavement.
Yours sincerely,
J.A.Simmons (Lieutenant)
P.S. Unfortunately your son's personal property was destroyed by the shell that killed him.

Bertha sank slowly onto the small front wall feeling strangely numb. Sarah Southern walked quickly round the corner to bring John from the Smithy. Sarah's youngest would have to be fetched from school and William would need to know. Mr. Thompson kindly phoned Albert at the St. Anne's branch and told him to come home by the next train. At least the journey gave him time to think. He had felt rather hurt by Joe's letter to him, hinting that he ought to become directly involved in the war but how could he leave the family at this time? Over the weekend he discussed the problem with Kath-

Albert Foxley's grave lies in the French National Cemetery at Vauxbuin.

leen, who wanted him to go to avenge Joe's death, but did not want to lose the young man she had grown to love. The deciding factors were Bertha's grief, John's obvious depression and desolation at the loss. He would put his future plans on hold until the family had, to some extent, assuaged its grief.

During the summer, another six local boys, all from Joe's battalion, lost their lives on the Somme. Bertha gave what comfort she could to their mothers, especially Sarah Southern, who had again lost a son. Albert, however, watched and waited. He was determined to 'do his bit' and finally, at the beginning of November, he told Kathleen that the time had come. He enlisted that week in the Royal Field Artillery and was soon posted to basic training camp. John comforted Bertha. As a gunner Albert, would not be in the front line.

He'd simply be firing from the back. Obviously it would not be so dangerous. In December 1917, his training was complete. Albert was given two weeks' leave prior to his departure for France. He assured the family that he would soon return and there just might be a wedding to celebrate. Kathleen blushed – they were not engaged but they had a deep understanding. In his early letters home, Albert left the family in no doubt that, although conditions were trying, he was doing well. He was truly appreciative of the parcels from Bertha and the family but he never mentioned fighting.

The War Office telegram arrived on Tuesday morning, the 23rd April 1918, quickly followed by an Artillery Officer's letter:

> Dear Mr. and Mrs. Foxley,
> It is my painful duty to inform you that your son, Albert, died in hospital as a result of a railway accident.
> The accident happened at one am on the morning of the 14th April and he died during that day in hospital. We were on the move at the time, going to a new part of the front and it was only yesterday, the 15th, that intimation reached us of his death.
> He had been in my section since he joined the unit and he was a splendid fellow. Always cheery and willing, no matter what job he was called upon to do, and, whatever the circumstances, he always went about it cheerfully.
> His loss will be mourned by us all from the Commanding Officer to the lowest ranks. Please accept the sincerest condolences of his comrades, his N.C.O.s. and his Officers.

That Sunday the remnants of the Foxley family made their way to St. John's Church, there to receive the deep-felt condolences of their neighbours and to hear the words of

The Lost Boys of Lostock

the Reverend Uttley in a special memorial service for Jack Kelly, John Bladon and, of course, Albert Foxley. Tucked away in the 'In Memoriam' column of the Northwich Guardian later that month appeared the following:-

> Sleep my dear Albert, in your far-off grave.
> A grave I shall never see.
> But as long as life and memory last
> I shall always think of thee.
> Sadly missed by Kathleen.

Albert's remains were buried in the 'Cimetière des Fusilles', a French Military Cemetery at Vauxbuin between Soissons and Paris. When the French Graves Service in 1922 built the French National Cemetery at Vauxbuin, all remains from a large number of graveyards in the area were moved to it. Albert had found his 'far-off grave'. The shell that ended Joe's life had done its work to maximum effect. He is one of the 20,000 officers and men who fell in the area north of Lens and have no known grave. He is commemorated on the Loos Memorial.

The last of the Foxley boys, William, never left home. He stayed with Bertha and John until, at the relatively young age of 48, he died in February 1936 and was buried in St. John's Churchyard, Lostock Gralam. The Foxley line was ended.

No grave for Joe Foxley. He is commemorated on the Loos Memorial.

The 'Canadians' Come Home

IN THE first week of January 1910, the initial advertisements appeared:

IN THE EMPIRE – UNDER THE FLAG
Get a Piece of the Earth .... in CANADA

The targets – simple. British farm workers and domestic servants, for whom there was unlimited work and, as a major inducement, 160 acres of government land FREE to any settlers of more than two years standing. The advertisements appeared weekly throughout that year, supported by a Canadian Government backed scheme whereby established settlers paid recruiting visits to the UK to 'spread the word'.

One such gentleman was a Mr. Charles Davis who, along with his family, had emigrated to Saskatchewan from Cheshire in 1872. Accompanied by his wife, he was now (February 1910) on a one month lecture tour speaking about the 'Golden West', advising the ambitious and willing young men of their prospects in 'Britain's nearest overseas dominion' being only one week by sea from Liverpool. The Davises painted a glowing picture. After their hard work on both building the Canadian Pacific Railway and on the land, they, along with their two sons, now owned some 1,200 acres of wheat and oats, 19 horses and 30 head of cattle, and all were in extremely robust health because of the superb Canadian climate. Mr. Davis pointed out to his enthralled audience that farm labourers were in great demand and he had experienced real difficulty hiring help during the recent harvest even though he was offering three dollars a day (approx. twelve shillings and sixpence). Mrs. Davis offered the young women even more. Whilst there was plenty of work for domestic servants, there were many comparatively young men in good positions on the lookout for suitable life partners!!

For some weeks the young were bombarded by both the written and spoken word. Apart from the standard advertisements, articles appeared on life in Canada, how to build your first log cabin, education, agriculture etc. Even their Eminences, the Archbishops of Canterbury and York, wrote to the press appealing for funds to support their missionaries (an intended 50 men for each of the next 10 years) to cater to the religious needs of the rapidly growing population of Canada. Almost fortnightly there were accounts published of Liverpool sailings to the Dominion, as in early March when the S.S. Virginia sailed full of young men and women, encouraged by the prospects of the pioneering life after the failure of trade in Lancashire and Cheshire. At this time the opportunities became limitless. Huge demands were being made, not only in farming but in coal mining, railway construction, building and, as always, domestic help. Frank Oliver, the Canadian Minister of the Interior, had adopted an aggressive immigration policy to meet the needs of his totally underpopulated country as early as 1906. He had increased the number of Booking Agents in Britain to over 100 and paid them two dollars for every British labourer recruited and placed in Ontario, Quebec and British Columbia. So successful was the policy that in the four year period 1910 -13, over half a million young Britons went to seek their fortunes in the Dominion.

A number of young men from Lostock Gralam were seriously tempted. In comparison with the drudgery at the chemical works, life in the Golden West, as portrayed in all of the advertisements and lectures, offered an earthly paradise. Early in the spring of 1910, Billy Johnson of Station Road reached his decision, assured his family that he would be back as soon as he had made his fortune and left for Liverpool. Within two weeks, he found himself in the 'quickly-growing' Preston, Ontario. Work here was plentiful, bunk-house accommodation available and cheap for single men, and a considerable number of emigrants were willing simply 'to give it a go'. When news of the European conflict reached Canada, Billy was amongst the first to volunteer to go back to fight for King and Country. He joined the 1st Western Ontario Battalion in August 1914, which was immediately assigned a place in the 1st Canadian Infantry Division, which arrived in England in October for a short period of training on Salisbury Plain.

Another amongst their number was William Wilson Drinkwater. William had been emotionally ripped asunder in 1912 with news filtering back by mail from the Lostock and Northwich boys who had sailed for the Dominion in the preceding two years. None had returned so far, beaten by the way of life. Most wrote only of the superb climate and prospects on offer. William, however, had a dilemma, in the shape of pretty Polly Davies from Church Street in the nearby village of Wincham, his childhood sweetheart. After much heart-searching the pair agreed – William would go to Canada, establish himself and send for Polly at the earliest opportunity. To seal their pact, the lovers became engaged a few days before William sailed for Toronto in the summer of 1913. Despite his early success in farming there, his stay was to be truncated by events back home and he joined the 4th Central Ontario Battalion of the 1st Canadian Infantry Division in August 1914. His training pattern followed that of Billy Johnson, with one exception. At Christmas 1914 he was granted two weeks' leave during which, on 5th January 1915, he married his beloved Polly at St. John's Church in Lostock. She worried about William's imminent visit to the trenches but was reassured that he would soon be back to collect her and to introduce her to the wonders of Toronto. One week later, William rejoined his battalion, leaving a tearful Polly on Northwich railway station. They were never to meet again.

William landed in France in February 1915, with the six hundred and ten officers and over seventeen thousand, two hundred men of the First Canadian Division. After a short period in base camp the troops were rushed forward to stem the German advance outside Ypres. On the twenty-second of April, the Commander of the German 4th Army, Archduke Albrecht, gave permission for the first ever use of chlorine gas in warfare, along a five mile front, causing a mass retreat of the French and Algerian troops, gasping for air. The German forces quickly advanced towards Ypres, only to be stopped in their tracks by a combined force of British and Canadian soldiers, which numbered less than half of their German opponents. In the fierce hand-to-hand fighting which followed, some 6,000 men, over one third of the Canadian force, was lost in a forty-eight hour period. William Drinkwater was amongst them, killed near St. Julien. His battlefield grave disappeared in later conflict and he is commemorated on the Menin Gate at Ypres.

Despite their appalling losses, the 1st Canadian Division, after a brief period in rest camp, were again soon locked in battle with the enemy – this time in support of the failing British attack at Aubers Ridge. Within weeks they had moved on to Festubert where they suffered a further two thousand, five hundred casualties and, undaunted, found themselves outside Givenchy in the second week of June. On the 15th of that month Billy Johnson and the men of Canada's very first unit of enlisted men, the 1st Western Ontario Battalion, attacked the German strongpoint known as 'Dorchester', outside Givenchy. In their midst was forty-eight-year-old regular officer, Captain Frederick William Campbell, whose bravery on that day was to bring him a Victoria Cross, awarded posthumously, because, along with 400 other Canadians, he was to be a casualty of extremely bloody trench fighting. Billy Johnson, too, was to make the supreme sacrifice on June 15th. In a letter received by his Mum, back in Lostock Gralam, a fellow combatant described how Billy had met his end:

> We had won the Germans' trench after a real dust-up, with a lot of our lads left in no-man's-land. We had just started to realise that our ammunition was running out when the Germans came back at us and we had to run for it. Me and Billy made it but then we heard a wounded mate of ours shouting near the German wire. Billy insisted on going back for him, even though we all said that it was too dangerous.
> I am sad to tell you that he just got shot and we had to go and rescue him. He lasted for twelve hours but told us he had no pain. Billy's last words to me were, "Tell them at home I did my duty".

Billy's remains were lost in the ensuing fierce fighting but he is honoured both on the Vimy Memorial and, poignantly, on the Johnson Family's headstone in St. John's Churchyard in Lostock.

Among the last of the Lostock Canadians to enlist was Tom Davenport, who had joined the small exodus in 1912. Tom was a craftsman whose skills as a joiner- cum-wheelwright were much appreciated. He had been apprenticed from school to Mr. Dutton of Northwich and had enjoyed a pleasant enough life in the village. He was an enthusiastic member of the Vicar's wife, Mrs. Tudor-Evans', Bible Class and was held

The Front Line trench manned by Canadians.

in considerable esteem. However, his ambition too had been fuelled by the news from the Dominions. The Booking Agent in Northwich had guaranteed him fame and fortune because of his known skills and Tom's head had been easily turned. In April 1912, aged 26, he had sailed for Canada. His early months in Canada, however, were to prove just as difficult as he could have anticipated. He had soon found employment on the Great Canadian Pacific Railway and his quiet, determined manner quickly won him friends amongst his co-emigrants. He had survived his first Canadian winter with aplomb when a letter with a Northwich postmark disturbed his calm; his mother had written to tell him of the untimely death of his dad, John, whose work as a blacksmith had influenced Tom's own choice of trade. Within a few short months Tom had made arrangements to return to Europe by joining the 31st Alberta Battalion of the Canadian Infantry. This was to form part of the 2nd Canadian Division that crossed the Atlantic and encamped on Salisbury Plain in May 1915. A short furlough allowed Tom to pay a fleeting visit to his mum in Lostock before the Division joined its vanguard 1st Division in France that September. Tom's first year on the Western Front was not without incident. After the initial trench-digging practice, preparing for the terrain to be defended, the 31st Albertas first saw action at the St. Éloi Craters, where three weeks of severe fighting left the whole brigade seriously damaged – but already gaining a reputation as fierce fighting men. Tom left the trenches with a damaged hand but, after a brief convalescence, was able to rejoin his mates in time for the historic attack on Flers and Courcelette on 15th September 1916. The battle entered the history books because of the first use of Churchill's 'land battleships' in war – the tanks.

Pte. W. Johnson, Pte. W. Drinkwater, Pte. T. Davenport

The triumph at Courcelette is still remembered in Canada with districts, villages and street signs so named in memory of the 8,000 Canadians who died there in the six days of fighting. To this day, Courcelette lives large in Canadian memory. A local farmer, in 1998, laying drainage pipes, discovered the remains of a soldier some feet below the surface. Because of his metal 'dog tags', he was soon identified as Private J. McArthur of the Canadian Infantry, who had been killed in September 1916. Perhaps even more poignantly, he had been a member of the 31st Alberta Battalion – Tom's 'lot'! Tom had his own reason for remembering the successful attack – a serious thigh wound. Even this had its benefits in that it brought his repatriation to a military hospital in Kent and, furthermore, it allowed a fleeting visit from Elizabeth, his mum. By the spring of 1917 Tom was sufficiently recovered to be able to rejoin the 31st in their meticulous preparations for the proposed attack on the German-held strongpoint of Vimy Ridge, essential for the protection of their mines and factories still in full production on the Dovai Plain. On Easter Monday, April 9th, at 5.30am, for the first time in their history, all four Canadian Divisions attacked together in driving sleet and snow across a thoroughly mangled terrain, going head-first into enemy machine guns. The Ridge was taken and, years later, one of the senior Canadian officers at the time was to say:

> It was Canada from the Atlantic to the Pacific on parade. I thought then . . . that in those few minutes I witnessed the birth of a nation.

Tom Davenport was not to enjoy the experience of being at that birth. He was killed in the first wave of the attack and is today remembered on the Vimy Memorial which towers above the Ridge, commemorating over 60,000 young Canadians who made the ultimate sacrifice in World War I.

Burial of two British soldiers on the Battlefield.
(John Chesworth Collection)

Lostock's Subalterns

GEORGE Marlow and William Hesketh may have been born on opposite sides of the fence, socially speaking, but their short lives (and ultimate deaths) put them in a proximity which might have made them cousins. Born only a few houses apart, on Manchester Road, in the latter years of the nineteenth century, they had both prospered in their early years, winning places at the prestigious Sir John Deane's Grammar School in Northwich. William had enjoyed a comfortable, if somewhat refined, childhood, at Highfields House, an imposing property at the heart of the village, surrounded by the high walls which his father, William, owner of the family corn mill, deemed appropriate to a man of his standing. Indeed, two generations of the Hesketh family figured prominently in the life of the community, not only as employers, but also as committed Methodists who had built the two chapels; one in 1877 in Lostock Green and the other, in 1895, in Lostock Gralam.

Following the example of both his grandfather and father (for many years a steward on the Northwich Methodist Circuit), young William, at only 18 years of age, not only preached in both chapels but soon became secretary and teacher to Lostock Green Sunday School. At the age of twenty, William was appointed to the honorary post of treasurer of 'The Worn-Out Ministers' Fund'. On leaving school, William had immediately joined the family business, Hesketh's Corn Mill in Lostock, very much as a junior in the mill to learn the business from the bottom upwards. After two years' education in the process of flour milling, he was transferred to the mill office where he would learn the commercial side of the business. William's natural friendliness and unassuming enthusiasm for the job made him popular with workmates and, when he purchased his first motor cycle, early in 1912, he was ready to cast his career net even further as a traveller for the family business. He was frequently to be seen on the road between Highfields and Plumley, where he was soon to become engaged to Mary Johnson of Oakfield House. This almost idyllic lifestyle, like that of so many of the men of his generation, was to come to an abrupt halt. William was among the first to enlist. Typically, he offered his services, not as expected by many who knew him, as a commissioned officer, but as a private soldier in the 17th Manchesters, informally known as the 2nd Manchester Pals' Battalion.

The Battalion had crossed to France in November 1915 as part of the 30th Division, heading for the huge build-up of men, weaponry and supplies being assembled in the region of the River Somme, ready for the planned 'Big Push' in the summer of 1916.

On July 1st, William was part of the successful attack on the village of Montauban, one of the few 'victories' on that dreadful day. Over 57,000 men fell on the Somme that day, of whom more than one third would never rise again. Amongst the fortunate ones was William, who received a severe bullet wound below his knee. After treatment at an advanced dressing station, he was transported for treatment back to the United Kingdom and, to his family's delight, was eventually hospitalized at Rock Ferry, near Birkenhead, where he was to spend two months. Amongst his many visitors was his sister, Sissie, a V.A.D. (Voluntary Aid Detachment) nurse, serving at the military hospital in Knutsford. No doubt she was just as delighted as the rest of the family when William announced, during his short recuperation at Highfields, that he was to apply for a commission when he was fully fit. In Plumley, Mary worried privately. Conversation over family meals had touched on the simple fact that, whilst large numbers of private soldiers were being killed and wounded, the number of subaltern casualties was much higher in comparative terms.

Having completed his officer training and having said his goodbyes, resplendent in his new tailored uniform, William left Lostock Gralam to join his assigned regiment - the Cheshires. In April 1917 he reported to the 10th Battalion as a brand new Second Lieutenant, welcomed by many familiar faces from both the old school and the old village. The 10th Cheshires had been engaged in serious trench raiding in mid-February 1917, resulting in the deaths of two young officers, whilst two others had been seriously wounded. William was one of the replacements. On the 6th June William posted his last letter home. Its tone was bright and cheerful and typically optimistic about the future. However there was a warning note:

> This might be my last letter for some time as we are about to move up to the front line in the next few days. You are not to worry, Mum, as we are a strong, confident group and, with God's good grace, we shall be triumphant.

In fact, the Cheshires were represented by four battalions in the major attack around Messines, which began on the morning of 7th June. The 10th Cheshires' War Diary shows one officer having been seriously wounded. In his first engagement William was immediately removed from the line. He clung to life for just two days at a casualty clearing station near Bailleul. On the 9th June, he expired from his wounds, ignorant of the fact that he had taken part in one of the truly successful British attacks of the War.

He is one of over 4,000 allied troops buried in Bailleul Community Cemetery Extension.

The death and funeral of George Marlow would, no doubt, have been known to William Hesketh. Whilst William was recovering from his wounds in the late summer of 1916, news was reaching the village of the dreadful accident that had happened to George.

Lt. W. Hesketh

George senior, a labourer at Brunner's, had decided early in his marriage that his children would, if possible, enjoy a less arduous lifestyle than his own. Hence he was delighted when young George won a place at Sir John Deane's Grammar School where he prospered. Having won a place at Crewe Teachers' College as a trainee teacher, George was to show some considerable ability, not least on the football field where he represented both the College and also the well-established local Witton Albion Football club. After his training period, George was happy to obtain a teaching post in Weaste, near Salford.

The pressure on the young men of that time was so great, however, that George taught for a mere two months. In December 1915, he attested and applied for a commission in the British Army. Whilst George senior was probably pleased to hear of his son's acceptance as a trainee officer, perhaps his delight was tinged with a little sadness that he had not followed a family tradition of applying for a posting to the Senior Service. After all, George's great grandfather had brought real credit to the family when, as a junior midshipman on HMS Victory, he had helped to carry the mortally wounded body of Admiral Nelson to the cockpit where he had eventually expired. Great grandpa had returned from the Navy after meritorious service, and enjoyed his 'rising pension' from the Admiralty until he died aged 99. George senior, proud of the old man's fame, had specially visited the great warship, had stood on the brass plate marking the spot where Nelson had fallen and traced the steps across which the wounded Admiral's body had been carried. George's life was to be much shorter than his great grandfather's and his death much less heroic than that of the great naval hero.

Having trained for some five months at the Number 3 Officer Cadet Battalion Training Camp, George was commissioned to the 6th Battalion of the Lancashire Fusiliers, but first he was to assist with the training of soldiers even less experienced than himself at Bramshott Camp in Hampshire. Within a few weeks of his arrival George was sent to assist Lieutenant Norman Brown with the instruction of about twenty new recruits in the art of live-bomb throwing. Towards the end of the session, in which George, alone in an adjacent trench, was acting as 'spotter', a mis-thrown grenade hit the top of the sandbag divide and fell sideways into his vicinity. George tried to run for cover but managed no more than three or four paces before the inevitable explosion occurred. Norman Brown explained to the Coroner how he had found George bleeding badly from a wound above his right knee but quite conscious. While George smoked a cigarette, Brown removed his puttees and boots, applied a tourniquet and dressing to stop the bleeding, simultaneously despatching runners to fetch a doctor and an ambulance.

The nearest hospital was within the area of the camp, run by the Canadian Army Medical Corps. A senior physician, Major G. H. Gilmore, described the nature of George's wounds, which were septic at the time of his admission on August 15th. The serious nature of George's wounds was described in a letter from the ward sister to his parents. who immediately arranged to visit their son. They arrived on 23rd August to discover that George had already undergone three operations but was holding his own. Indeed, the following morning his condition

George Marlow's grave in St John's churchyard, Lostock Gralam.

had improved to the extent that George senior felt sufficiently confident to return to Lostock leaving his wife to give comfort to their son. Sadly, on the evening of the 26th gangrene was discovered and poor George had his leg amputated. Next morning he was comparatively bright and cheerful. Mum sat with him throughout the day but popped out for ten minutes as George drifted into sleep. He never woke up.

The Lost Boys of Lostock

T. Arthur Cowley, the Honorary Secretary of the Northwich and District War Fund (a man who was highly supportive of the Lostock families during the War) arranged for George to be buried in his local churchyard with full military honours. The village prepared itself for the last journey of one of its own on Saturday 2nd September. Curtains were drawn at every house; every shop was shuttered. The people left their houses and quietly lined Manchester Road from outside the Marlow family's home to the front of St. John's as George made his final journey. The coffin, draped with the Union Jack and with George's belt, cap and sword laid on top, was carried by six Lancashire Fusilier Sergeants and two Sergeant Majors. Six Fusiliers and three Cheshire officers followed the bier with swords reversed in their scabbards. A large number of family members were followed to the church by several soldiers on either munition duties at Lostock Works or on leave. The 1st Lostock and 7th Northwich Boy Scouts paraded, as did representatives from Crewe College, George's old schools and, of course, his church. The Reverend M.P. Uttley spoke of George and, at greater length, of the need to go to church in these difficult times. After the congregation had sung the well-known hymns, accompanied by George's great pal, Jim Hoole, on the organ, a bugler played the Last Post and six Lancashire Fusiliers fired three volleys over the grave as George was lowered to his final resting place in the churchyard. He shares his grave with his brother, Harold, who had died in infancy in 1912 and, eventually, with both of his parents. There is no CWGC headstone.

> The short history of Charles Victor Blain, who enjoyed his 2nd Lieutenancy for but a few days, is included in the chapter headed 'Boundary Street'.

The Lost Boys of Lostock

The Back-to-Back Terraces by St. John's

Arthur Street

The only recorded father and son enlistments in Lostock Gralam were those of 41-year-old William Southern in 1915 and his 18-year-old son, John, who joined up in February 1916. William and Emily Southern, with their two children, were the first occupants of No. 14 Arthur Street in 1902. By 1915, the family had developed somewhat to count three sons and seven daughters. One wonders whether his labouring life at Ammonia Soda and his Sunday morning walk through Lostock Hollows to the calm of the Methodist Chapel in Lostock Green afforded William sufficient refuge from the clamour in Arthur Street. No doubt fired by patriotism but possibly encouraged by a short 'holiday' from his family, William joined the 10th Cheshires. As the new 'man of the house', 17-year-old John soon followed his dad to the recruiting office and was assigned to the 3rd Cheshires in February 1916.

Pte. W. Southern

The careers of the Southerns followed similar paths. Because of his age, William was posted to various locations in the United Kingdom, until heavy losses at the Somme in 1916 led to his being sent, in November, as a replacement for one of the many Cheshires who had fallen in that conflict. William's career at the front was to be short-lived. In a sharp bout of German artillery fire, the front line trenches were shattered and the elder Southern died of his wounds, in a Casualty Clearing Station, on Christmas Eve 1916.

John did his brief war service in the 3rd (Special Reserve) Battalion, which spent the whole of the war based in the UK, mainly guarding the docks at Liverpool and acting as a depot for the Cheshire Regiment as a whole. After a mere ten months of service, John was found to have heart problems and was discharged on 29th December 1916, arriving back in Lostock just as the news of his father's death reached Arthur Street.

Some ten miles south of Ypres, near the village of Ploegstreert, in Tancrez Farm

The Lost Boys of Lostock

Cemetery, William lies at rest, mourned by Emily and their ten children.

Fitton Street

No. 6: A letter was received by Infantry Records at Shrewsbury on 15th December 1915:

> James Bramhall, brother of John of the 6th South Lancashire Regiment, is very anxious to know if you have any further information concerning his brother and has asked me to write on his behalf. I saw, from letters at home, that Private Bramhall was wounded on August 10th and posted as 'missing' in November.
> I feel it is a forlorn hope but I promised to write to satisfy the brother.
> Yours very faithfully,
> Reverend W. Livesey

It was indeed a forlorn hope – 25-year-old John, one of the siblings of Samuel Bramhall, was already dead. He had enlisted in the South Lancs. in November 1914 and, after training, had sailed from Avonmouth on the S.S. Amonia in July 1915, bound for Gallipoli, where, on 4th August, they had landed on Anzac Beach. A fierce battle, to take

The Helles Memorial.

the heights of Sari Bair above Sulva Bay, ensued during which, only six days after landing, John Bramhall was killed in action. Like so many of his mates, his body was never found and, along with nearly 21,000 Commonwealth soldiers, his name rests in perpetuity on the 30 metres high Helles memorial, which stands on the tip of the Gallipoli Peninsula.

John's younger brother, Sam, was to fare better. A 'Saturday Night Soldier' in the Terriers, or the 1/5th Battalion of the Cheshire Regiment, since 1912, Sam survived the bloodshed and was discharged from the Army in 1919, proudly being able to wear the Military Medal.

Herbert Street

No. 1: Little information is available on Thomas Hall, who had moved with his family into No. 1 Herbert Street just before the Outbreak. He does, however, hold the distinction of being, at 44 years of age, the second oldest Lostock resident to lose his life whilst a serving soldier. Thomas served in the Northumberland Fusiliers and, whilst there is no record of his life in the military, he died in mid-January 1920, in the 1st London Hospital in Camberwell. He now lies in St. John's Churchyard, his wife, Jessie, alongside him, having survived him by some thirty years. Despite his CWGC headstone, Thomas is not recorded on the church's Memorial Cross.

No. 6: The oldest Lostock Gralam man to enlist in the British Army was 43-year-old Joseph Garner of 6 Herbert Street. Joseph was an old soldier in every sense of the word. As an 18-year-old farm labourer, born and bred in Lostock, he had sought a more exciting, better paid life early in January 1889 by enlisting in the Cheshire Regiment on a seven year commitment. After nearly two years of training, he sailed for the Indian Frontier in November 1890, returning home after six years' service. Within three months Ellen Cawley, a local girl,

Thomas Hall's headstone in St John's churchyard.

became Mrs. Garner. The call-to-arms caused Joe to re-enlist in 1899 for the South African campaign, where he won four medals, one in each of Orange Free State, the Transvaal, Africa and Johannesburg.

On returning to civilian life in 1903, Joe joined the morning walk to Ammonia Soda – and produced three sons with Ellen. The heavy manual work was, however, to prove injurious to his health in the long term. At the Outbreak, Joe immediately dusted off his equipment and headed for the recruiting office, no doubt with Ellen's protests ringing in his ears. His old regiment was pleased to accept his know-how and, early in 1915, he sailed with the 2nd Cheshires, an experienced battalion of seasoned troops, who had served with distinction in India. Their courage and determination stood them in good stead in the first Battle of Ypres in 1915 and Joe served his battalion well. However, trench life affected him badly and early in 1916, Joe found himself, suffering from chronic bronchitis and an aortic aneurysm, in the 24th General Hospital at Étaples, where he was to remain until he sailed, on the Hospital Ship, 'Brighton', for England in May 1916. Long stays in hospital at Cambridge and Eastbourne followed, with Ellen claiming a railway warrant to visit him on at least one occasion. Eventually, and ironically, Joe was transferred to work on munitions at Ammonia Soda in Lostock, but his stay was short-lived. His cough was permanent and shattering. Successive Medical Boards accepted that it was attributable to Military Service, which had also aggravated his aneurysm. Finally, at Chester War Hospital in March 1918, he was granted his military discharge and a 50% degree of disablement accepted. Joe's condition continued to deteriorate rapidly and a pensions tribunal in February 1919 accepted his disablement to be at a degree of 100%. By now he was housebound and, within three months, he was dead. He lies in St. John's Churchyard in Lostock, his grave marked by a CWGC headstone.

A CWGC headstone marks the grave of Joe Garner in St John's.

Tyne Cot, the world's biggest British Commonwealth Memorial.

Soldiers on leave outside the Black Greyhound at Four Lane Ends.

By the Side of the Church

School Lane

The great majority of the lost sons of Lostock Gralam had spent some time, in their formative years, walking along School Lane on their journeys to and from school. There were, in 1910, 37 houses in the Lane, largely inhabited by very young families. By the end of the Great War, from the twelve households with sons of enlistment age, nine had suffered casualties, seven of whom had made the supreme sacrifice.

No. 3: The Goulding family were born and bred Lostock residents. They had lived in School Lane since 1900, enjoying the proximity of the schools, shops, church and pubs. Pass Goulding had found life difficult providing for Rachel and their six children until, over a period of three years, John Kinsey, a local farmer, had offered some small salvation when, as each of the Goulding boys in turn left school, they went as live-in farm hands; Frank as a waggoner; George as a cow man and Robert as a hackney lad, on Hulse Farm, Lach Dennis, some two miles from School Lane.

By the Outbreak, Frank had joined his old school chums labouring at the Alkali works and, on 31st August 1914, enlisted with them in the 10th Cheshires. His war followed that battalion's path until, in the trenches in April 1916, he received a gunshot wound to his back, possibly from a sniper's rifle and, after treatment in France, was shipped home to a Military Hospital in Holloway, where he was to remain until his recovery and transfer to the Mediterranean Force in October of that year. A serious bout of malaria brought Frank's war to an end in April 1918, and he was discharged with a 40% disability pension worth eleven shillings per week, and a Silver War Badge.

His younger brother, George, was to fare even worse. By the time he had gone to enlist, the 10th Cheshires was full. The alternative, the 11th Battalion, spent most of its time training alongside the 10th so the brothers saw each other regularly. Their preparations over, they sailed for France within twenty four hours of each other and prepared, like so many in the New Army, for the 'Big Push'. Despite the news of Frank's departure with his 'blighty' wound, George steeled himself for what was to come. His battalion was heavily involved in the catastrophe of the early days of the Somme battle and George's luck ran out on 29th August when, in heavy trench-fighting near Pozières, he was killed. He lies in Pozières British Cemetery. Young Robert's boss had successfully pleaded for his farmhand's exemption from military service because of his work of National Importance; a small compensation for mum, Rachel.

No. 17: A small domestic tragedy found its roots at the home of Joseph and Harriet Alcock when family member, Mary Jane Baddeley, joined them in the spring of 1890 from Egremont, Liverpool, accompanied by her very newly-born son. St. John's register of baptisms for July 1890 shows Mary Jane as unmarried. The local school's register from April 1907 records Joseph Alcock as Harry Sidney Baddeley's 'parent', although the 1901 Census return lists the boy as grandson to the Alcocks. After school, Harry worked for C.H. Leather in Sale, Manchester, as a provisioner until September 1914. He attested and joined his hometown regiment, the King's Liverpools, and was assigned to the 18th Battalion. Harry's service record illustrates his qualities as a soldier. His first experience of total war came on 1st July 1916, when, in the major offensive on the Somme, he and his pals were part of the highly successful 30th Division's attack on Montauban. Such were the losses that he was immediately promoted to fill one of the many vacancies as a paid Lance Corporal. His enthusiasm for soldiering resulted in his receiving extra training in anti-gas defences at his Divisional Training Camp and, in spite of his spending time in a Field Ambulance with a gunshot wound to his head, he was soon to be awarded a good conduct badge on completion of two years' service. As part of his reward he was granted two weeks' leave in the UK. It was to be his last sight of the old country. Soon after returning to the 18th Battalion, Harry received a further promotion to full Corporal in May 1917 and, after some terrible fighting near

Stretcher bearers in knee-deep mud on Pilckem Ridge.

Ypres in June, he won a citation which was written, oddly enough, by his Company Commander on Army Form B122, which was used to record offences committed and punishments received by the troops.

It simply records, under Harry's name, rank and number: Beneath, in the same hand, is written: 'Killed in Action 31-7-17'.

Harry and over eighty of his 18th Battalion pals were killed on the same day at the battle for Pilckem Ridge, just outside Ypres. Many of them were hastily buried in nearby Sanctuary Wood, but, after the War, when smaller cemeteries were evacuated, Harry's remains were finally laid to rest at Hooge Crater Cemetery, some three miles east of Ypres. The CWGC details record that he was the son of 'Mrs' Mary Jane Baddeley of Lostock Gralam.

Nos. 21 and 23: Arthur Harriman, at 21, and Tommy Wright, at 23, were to experience similar histories. Arthur, a regular soldier, was rushed to France with the 1st Cheshires, was captured at Mons and spent much of the following four years writing to the philanthropical Mrs Buckley, at the Black Greyhound, either thanking her for her parcels or listing the items he needed in the next one! He was repatriated in December 1918. Tommy had joined the 17th Manchesters in November 1915 and was detailed to France in the spring of 1916. Within a very short time he was captured in a trench raid and spent the rest of his war in Germany, before being allowed home in December 1918. Tommy's peace was to be short- lived. In August 1919 he was killed by a collapse of marl at the Brunner Mond works.

No. 25: The 16th Battalion was in the front line of the Brigade . . . The night of the 21st/22nd (of October 1917) was bitterly cold and rain fell heavily. The men were perished. Unfortunately, rum and tea, which had been provided, did not reach the Battalion as the enemy kept up a strong barrage fire all night. At 5.30am an advance started. The state of the ground can be imagined when it is learnt that the pace was 100 yards in eight minutes. The whole ground was one mass of shell holes, each containing about a foot of water. Even at this slow pace the troops had the greatest difficulty keeping up with (their own) barrage. Still, the objectives were reached. Then began a long day's struggle, dealing first with unconquered pill-boxes (concrete machine-gun posts) and enemy counter-attacks . . . (that day) the 16th lost a total of 9 officers and 327 men. *Crookenden*

Pte. G. Riley

One of those men was 29-year-old George Riley, who was both badly wounded and taken prisoner. George had taken his bride, Hannah, to live in School Lane, quite close to his job at Ammonia Soda and convenient for all of the facilities on offer in Lostock. They had prospered in the village, with George playing regularly for Tabley Football team and Hannah producing four healthy children by the time of his enlistment in July 1915, when his service record shows that he was 'Fit for Home Service only' and posted to the 3rd Cheshires, a Home Defence Battalion, guarding the Isle of Man. However, as the carnage on the Western Front proceeded at a pace, George was posted first to the 13th Battalion and, within two months, to the 16th, in which he was to last but five days. Hannah received a postcard from him on 12th. November, telling her that he had been shot in his thigh and arm and was now a guest of Germany. Then . . . nothing! With the assistance of J. Arthur Cowley she had to endure three long months of wondering before she received a letter from the Red Cross in Geneva informing her that George had died of his wounds in Kriegslaz Military Hospital in Ghent on 25th November. A pension of 33s.9d. (approx. £1.66) per week was granted to Hannah, who was to leave School Lane with her children, in the autumn of 1919, as the new Mrs. Stagg of Northwich.

George lies forever in Ghent City Cemetery.

No. 27: In March 1923, Bill Turner was admitted to the Derby County Asylum in Mickleover suffering from manic depressive psychosis and psychopathic inferiority. His army service record classified him as 100% disabled but confirmed that there were no grounds for the award of a pension as his condition was non-attributable to his military service! Twenty-one-year old Bill had been sent to the Western Front with the 9th Cheshires, in March 1916. With his mates, he had arrived on the Somme in late May to prepare for the Big Push. His battalion was in first reserve on the 1st July, but next day they went 'over the top' at La Boiselle, trying to pick their way through the dead, dying and mutilated who had lain there overnight. With gunshot wounds to his chest, thigh and back, Bill was dragged in from No-Man's-Land and found himself, within one week, in a UK hospital, where he was to remain for four months. On his discharge, Bill was assigned as a replacement to the 12th Battalion fighting in Salonica, from where his family received a telegram informing them that he was in a casualty clearing station dangerously ill with influenza and pneumonia. Yet again, Bill pulled through and returned to England for demobilization in February 1919. Sadly, within months Bill, who had survived some personal catastrophes in both France and Serbia, was standing alongside his good old pal and near neighbour, Tommy Wright, at what the local paper called 'The Winnington Works Disaster', when Tommy was killed by a heap of falling marl. There is no record of how Bill came to be in Derby at the time of his committal to the local asylum. Perhaps taking to the road, like so many old soldiers did, was his way of dealing with real personal tragedy. Nevertheless, documents exist showing that Bill recovered. In 1933 he wrote to the Records Office at Shrewsbury seeking copies of his lost army discharge papers. He was back home in Lostock Gralam.

No. 39: Farm labourer, Sammy Carter, may well have attested in March 1915 on hearing that Nellie Cross was pregnant. Certainly Sammy had transferred from the 3rd to the 12th . Battalion, with whom he served in Salonica, between long periods bed-bound with malaria, before being posted to France. As a German bullet in the ankle in mid-1918 brought him to his knees, so an Army Order, initiated by Court Orders from the Northwich Petty Sessions Magistrates, finally caught up with him. Nellie was demanding her child's dues and was granted 6d. per day for its support, until it achieved 14 years of age. Whether Sammy fulfilled his obligations remains a mystery.

No. 45: 1916 was to prove a year of great sadness for Edith Hulme. Husband, John, was 'somewhere in France' with the 10th Cheshires, when, on April 10th she lost her ten-month -old son, Thomas, probably conceived on John senior's last leave before embarkation for France in September 1915. Indeed, it is probable that John never met his baby son.

In late July, Edith's grief was compounded by the news that John had been seriously wounded in the Somme battle at Bazentin and, after a brief stay in Casualty Clearing Station Number 49 at Gezaincourt, he expired. His last resting place is in Gezaincourt Community Cemetery extension. Edith's suffering was furthered early in January 1923, when her 12-year-old son, John, died. However, she was to find some happiness in 1927 when she married Thomas Jones, a widower, from four doors along School Lane.

No. 57: Following so many before them Arthur and Martha Hunt had brought their family, in the early 1900s, to the sound prospects offered by the Salt Industry in Lostock, from their original home in Thornton-le-Fylde in Lancashire. Their seven children had settled well at the Lostock schools, while Arthur had quickly found work in the Soda Ash Industry, where he was joined by James, his eldest son, in 1907. By 1911 the two

Gezaincourt Communal Cemetery Extension where lies John Hulme, of School Lane.

younger boys were similarly employed and with two of their four daughters also at work, the financial pressures on the Hunt family were relieved to the extent that they were able to move from No. 31, which had provided at best, restricted space, to a large house on School Lane, No. 57.

An abrupt end was brought to the family's comfortable existence in the autumn of 1914 when, within the first two weeks of November, the three sons enlisted. James joined the 12th Cheshires, Robert became a sapper in the Royal Engineers and Fred, barely seventeen-years-of-age, was allowed to join the 2/5th Cheshires, a territorial Battalion with whom he would remain in Britain until he reached eighteen-years-of-age. James and his battalion, after a brief stop in France, were sent to support the Serbians in their battles with the Turks and Bulgarians in late 1915, where most of the two years following were spent on pioneering duties. The climate was one of extremes but the biggest enemy was the marsh mosquito in the Struma Valley. Huge numbers of troops were struck down by malaria; James spending extended periods in the 43rd General Hospital in Salonika. In January 1918 he was transferred to England, eventually being assigned to the Labour Corps with whom he spent the duration. On his demobilization he was medically assessed as 70% disabled with malaria and related eye problems. Robert embarked for France with the 80th Field Company of the Royal Engineers in July 1915. He was to spend a very active period with his mates ensuring that the troops in the front line received maximum support, especially with bridge and road repairs. He was deeply involved in preparations for the Battle of the Somme, being part of the force that had some limited success in the early stages of that particular theatre near Montauban and remaining there until February 1917 when they were directed to Miraumont. In the two day operation of the 17th and 18th in a battle that was to decimate such fine regiments as the Royal Fusiliers and the Northamptons, Robert was to lose his life near Boom Ravine. His remains are buried in Regina Trench Cemetery at Grandcourt. He was twenty-years-of-age.

By pure coincidence younger brother Fred, now eighteen-years-of-age, received his overseas posting the day following Robert's death and sailed for France. He was transferred to the 1st Cheshires, whom he joined near Cambrai. Fred may have been the last of the Hunts to go to war but his achievements were quietly spectacular. His work as a stretcher bearer to 'B' Company won him much acclaim, including two promotions. Eventually, after his dedicated support of his front line comrades at Vimy Ridge in April 1917, he was awarded a Divisional Parchment Certificate for his general good conduct and devotion to duty in the trenches. The rare award of a second such certificate was made to Fred for his gallantry at Oppy Wood, on 28th June 1917, his name being recorded in the Battalion War Diary of 15th July. Further honour was bestowed on Fred when he was awarded the Military Medal for his unstinting efforts at Passchendaele in November 1917, his award being announced in the London Gazette of 28th January 1918. Fred's war was to come to a virtual end on the 4th August 1918 when he suffered under a German gas shell attack. After treatment in the 13th Field Ambulance and then the 54th Casualty Clearance Station, he was transported back to hospital in Leicester where he was to spend the ensuing three months until, on 15th November, just four days after the Armistice, he was granted recuperative leave at home.

Arthur and Martha Hunt had seen their three sons go to war: the eldest, James, came home with 70% disability: the second son, Bob, lies forever in the Regina Trench Cemetery on the Somme: the youngest son, Fred, returned a decorated hero but, probably emotionally scarred for life.

Smithy Lane
Probably the largest family to send its sons to war was the Sherlock family of Smithy Lane. In 1910, after twenty years of marriage, William and Mary Sherlock had given birth to Winifred, the thirteenth child of their union. Although three of their children had died in infancy, the surviving ten lived in the relatively spacious surroundings of six-

roomed No 1 Smithy Lane, in a degree of comfort greater than that normally enjoyed by an alkali labourer's family. After leaving Lostock Boys' School, William joined his father at Brunners as a chemical labourer, spending his leisure time on the bowling green and in the choir at St. John's Church. Unusually amongst his fellows William revealed an interest in politics by joining the fast-growing Primrose League, which had been established in 1881 to perpetuate the memory and principles of Prime Minister Benjamin Disraeli, whose favourite flower it was.

Pte. W. Sherlock

On 7th May 1915 William became the first member of the Northwich Branch to fall at the front. In November 1914, William, and his great pal, George Goulding, enlisted together at Northwich, their army numbers being consecutive. However, eager to see action, William answered the call of the 2nd Battalion, who were mobilized at Winchester and sailed for Le Havre in January 1915. The spring of 1915 saw the 2nd Cheshires fighting outside Ypres, alongside the 1st and the Territorials 1/5th. William's war was to be brief – a letter from his good friend, George Goulding, bearing the news to William and Mary, that their eldest son had been killed in the trenches at Frezenberg some four miles from Ypres town centre. George assured the family that William had had a proper burial at which he had assisted. As happened with so many of the front line graves William's was lost, probably destroyed by shell fire, in the later battles in the area. His name is to be found on the Menin Gate Memorial along with those of over 54,000 troops with no known grave.

A section of the Cheshire Regiment.
(John Chesworth Collection)

On Station Road

No. 52: The Regimental History describes the events of the 17th February 1917 as a 'raid', not as a full-blown 'battle', but merely as a 'raid'.

The attack had started at 9.45am after a sustained bombardment by howitzers, heavy guns and trench mortars on the German lines. However, the effect had not been as devastating as had been expected and, when some 200 Cheshires charged the German trenches, they were met by a storm of machine gun and small arms fire. The result of the 'raid' is best evidenced at the Berkshire's Cemetery Extension, some 5 miles south of Ypres, in which the Ploegsteert Memorial stands. Sixteen 10th Cheshires have their last resting places in Plot 1 of the former; whilst the names of a further thirty-four men, who have no known graves, are recorded on the latter. A total of fifty Cheshires lost their lives that day and another eighty men were seriously wounded. Some 'raid'!

Albert Kettle was born in Northwich and, after school, worked as a labourer with his older brother, bricklayer Ernest, at Brunners. At the Outbreak, the 24-year-old bachelor seized his chance for adventure and enrolled in the 8th Cheshires. After his training, he sailed with his mates, in November 1915, for Mesopotamia. The Battalion suffered appallingly from the heat, lack of fresh water, cholera and terrible skin complaints.

Albert, amongst many others, convalesced at home, after long periods in Field Hospitals. In late 1916, however, he managed to fill one of the many gaps in the sister regiment, the 10th Cheshires, which had been decimated by the bloodletting on the Somme. His stay in Flanders was to be eternal and he lies in a grave overlooking the Ploegsteert Memorial, which bears the name of his Lostock contemporary, Thornton Hickson, who was killed in the same raid.

No. 18: Herbert and Harold Miller were brothers, born of the same mother, but with unknown father/s. Their mother, Sarah, had moved from the family home in Lostock Green to stay with relatives in Holmes Chapel, some ten miles away, when her two sons were born, in 1898 and 1900 respectively; but, by the census of 1901, both boys were living back in Lostock as Thomas and Emily's grandsons. No service records exist for the boys and there is no reference to them in the local newspapers. However, each has an entry in the British Army Medal Roll Index, which helps us to confirm that:

Harold, born in 1900, was trained and based in France by September 1915, as a member of the 7th Battalion Norfolk Regiment. This would indicate that he was just fourteen years of age on enlistment, fifteen years old on embarkation and, after some three years' fighting, within four months of surviving the war when he died of wounds in pursuit of the retreating Germans in the final Allied advance in Artois. Harold is buried alongside 2nd Lieutenant Butler, aged 20, a fellow 7th Norfolks' man, in Auby Communal Cemetery. They occupy the sole war grave in that burial ground.

Brother Herbert had died some six weeks before his younger brother. He had been quickly recruited in July 1915 as a replacement into the 1st Cheshires, a regular battalion whose numbers had been decimated in the early months of the war. He had survived the horrors of the Somme and Ypres but his luck had ran out in the counter-offensive of early August 1918. He had been wounded severely and taken to the huge military hospital complex at Rouen, where he died on the 29th August 1918. He is buried in the St. Sever Cemetery Extension along with over eight thousand, six hundred Commonwealth troops.

No. 30: The Bladon family were both well established and well known in Lostock Green in August 1914. The father, James, was the local Police Sergeant, an officer of the Parish Church, treasurer to the successful football club and a keen member of the local Conservative party. His sons and daughters played their full part in village life. John's workmate and great pal was Jack Kelly of Renshaw Street. They bowled together for Lostock Alkali team, followed Lostock Gralam football team and, on 31st August 1914, enlisted within minutes of each other into the 10th Cheshires. In the months after his arrival in France John spent regular periods in both the Field Ambulance and hospital at Étaples suffering from chronic influenza. Eventually, in August 1917, he was seriously wounded in the left thigh by a bomb, spending some time in Bristol General Hospital.

Convalescing in Lostock Gralam offered little pleasure to John and he managed to convince the Medical Board that he was fit enough to return to France – this time to join the 15th Cheshires who were desperate for replacements. His service with them lasted but three months until, on 24th March 1918, he was killed in action in a counter-attack on Clery Ridge. No more than a couple of miles away, on the same day, Jack Kelly was meeting his end too. Neither of the two pals has a known grave. Jack's name is recorded on the Memorial at Arras whilst John Bladon is one of over 14,560 British and Commonwealth troops who are commemorated on the great Pozières Memorial.

No. 1: William and Mary Carter received two pieces of mail on the 15th April 1916: one from a Field Post Office in Mesopotamia; the other from the Army Records Office at Shrewsbury. The former, dated 4th April read: -

> Dear Mum and Dad,
> Just a line to let you know I am quite well. We have just had a rather warm time of it but we have had a bit of our own back too. Ted Gaunt (his next door neighbour) is alright and so is young Tom Bramhall, but we have all had some narrow escapes. Please let Mrs Buckley (the landlady at the 'Slow and Easy') know that all the Lostock boys in the 8th Cheshires are well.
>
> Your loving son,
> Charles

The letter from Shrewsbury was more ominous: -

> We regret to inform you that information from the War Office reports that 11239 Lance Corporal Charles Carter is posted as missing after an engagement at ***** on 9th April 1916.

The censored name was Fallhiya, an outpost on the marshy banks of the Tigris on the road to the besieged town of Kut in Mesopotamia.

On the 9th April 1916, the 8th Cheshires were severely depleted in the fighting; 2 officers were killed whilst 28 men were killed, 170 wounded and 7 forever lost. For months, William and Mary had no news of their eldest son despite their frequent appeals in the Northwich press and their letters to the War Office. Finally, in early July, Charles was officially declared to have been Killed in Action. His name is recorded on the Basra Memorial amongst over 40,500 men of the Commonwealth forces who died between 1914 and 1921 but who have no known graves.

No. 3: Fred Timmis qualified as a son of Lostock Gralam by his marriage to Minnie Gaunt in October 1916. He was born in Swanlow, Winsford, and had lived and worked, since leaving school, at Timperley Hall Farm in Altrincham. At the Outbreak, Fred had been granted special exclusion, as a farm labourer, from enlistment; but his growing relationship with Minnie in particular, and the Gaunt family as a whole, may have influenced his thoughts. Both of Minnie's elder brothers were serving in the military – Edward as a Sergeant Machine Gunner and young Harry in the 10th Cheshires. Fred may well have been slightly embarrassed now that he was the sole male of his generation at 3 Station Road, since his admittance to the Gaunt family home with his new bride.

Whatever his reasoning, 27-year-old Fred joined the 10th Cheshires in August 1915 and soon found himself at the Front as a stretcher bearer, where he received news that Minnie was pregnant. The baby, Edward, arrived on 7th March 1918 and, within three days, Fred was home, beginning a ten-day leave. His goodbye to Minnie and their new born son was exactly that. Fred left Station Road on the 24th March 1918 to rejoin his unit in France. The Battalion diary reports the action of 17th April 1918 as follows:

Pte. F. Timmis

> Holding the line at Wolfhock with the 2nd French Cavalry (dismounted). During the day the position was heavily shelled by guns of all calibre and also heavily bombarded with gas shells.

Fred Timmis was killed by a shell, his body lost forever. His name is recorded, along with those of 35,000 other officers and men of the United Kingdom and New Zealand, who died in this area and have no known grave, on the great Memorial at Tyne Cot, some five miles north-east of Ypres. Minnie and young Edward were granted a widow's pension of 21s.0d per week.

No. 17: By 1914, the working male members of the Snelson family were all firmly established in the local farming community – and all of them as waggoners. Father, William, worked for Mr. Warburton in Lostock; eldest son, George, for Mr. Newton at Allostock; second son, Thomas, at Plumley for Mr. Groves; and third son, Joseph, for Mr. Brandreth at Peover. Mum, Elizabeth, as was traditional, stayed at home with thirteen-year-old William junior and her two daughters, Lillian and Elizabeth. The family was able to afford a slightly larger home and moved to Station Road, within closer proximity to the village centre at the turn of the century. Generally, life for the Snelsons was probably more comfortable than that experienced by the great majority of Lostock families. But it was all to be radically changed in the summer of 1914. The inducements for a farm labourer to enlist were considerable – a 'holiday' in France; seven shillings a week all found; consolidated pay for the first four weeks of service; adventure; and the guarantee of your old job back at the end of hostilities; above all of course, the national surge of patriotism was overwhelming.

No wonder the Recruiting Offices were besieged in the first week of September. Thousands of men descended on the Town Hall in Manchester, demanding the King's shilling – amongst them 25-year-old George Snelson, who had resisted following the flow of Lostock men to the Cheshire Regiment. On Monday, September 7th 1914, George was assigned to the 4th Pals (officially the 19th {Service} Battalion of the Manchester Regiment). Over twelve months of training in England followed until, during a home leave in October 1915, he was able to tell the family that, at last, he was off to France as a member of the 90th Brigade, 30th Division, along with the lad who had stood behind him, next in line, at the Recruiting Office, and had since become his great friend, Fred Settle of Withington, Manchester.

They arrived at Le Havre on the 8th November 1915.

Younger brother, Thomas, preceded them by just five days. Along with brother, Joseph, he had arrived at the Recruitment Office in Northwich on the first day of January. Their army numbers are just five apart, but, for reasons unknown, they were assigned to different battalions of the Cheshires – Thomas to the 8th, which would serve much of the war in Mesopotamia after a brief sojourn in France, and Joseph to the 10th on the Western Front. In a period of just seven weeks the Snelson brothers had left the country – only one would return at the War's end. George fought on the Somme, most notably in the attack at Guillemont on 23rd July 1916 where well over half the Battalion were casualties, and in the great battles of 1917. Both he and his pal, Fred, were largely unscathed until the infamous attacks outside St. Quentin, on Manchester Hill, in March 1918.

Only one month before the 19th Manchesters, now seriously depleted, had been disbanded, their men being shared between the 16th and, in George's and Fred's cases, the 17th battalions. On 22nd March 1918, in the carnage around St. Quentin, near the significantly named Manchester Hill, George, Fred and other original 'Pals' were casualties. In the great German attack, many men were surrounded and marched away to spend the rest of the war in prison camps. In Lostock, the Snelson family could but hope that George was among their number, but the months passed without news. Finally, as the war ended, both George and his pal were 'assumed' killed on March 22nd. They have no known graves and are commemorated on the Monument at Poziers.

The Lost Boys of Lostock

There is never a good time to receive the news of the death of a loved one but, back at 17 Station Road, they were deep into grieving for Thomas. He had survived both the landings and the evacuation from Gallipoli and was sent with the 8th Cheshires to the totally ill-conceived operation in Mesopotamia in February 1916. The extremes of temperature led to Thomas spending various periods in hospital suffering from recurrent fever. His health continued to deteriorate until, in June 1918, he was repatriated suffering from pleurisy. A few weeks at home seemed to have restored Thomas to something approaching reasonable health. However, the Mesopotamian campaign being all but complete, he was posted to a home-based battalion, the 3rd Royal Welsh Fusiliers, stationed at Sarsfield barracks in Limerick, Ireland, from where a message was sent, in late October, informing the family of Thomas's serious problems with the strain of Spanish Influenza which was sweeping the world. Elizabeth immediately made arrangements to visit her son but, before she could take the first step on her journey, news arrived of Thomas's death. In a two-week period, fourteen men of the battalion were to succumb to the illness. All lie buried in King's Island, Limerick, a tiny, walled cemetery protected by a gentle caretaker working for the Irish Board of Works, who opens the locked gates on request, but, sadly, on no more than on one or two occasions in twelve months. Joseph Snelson, the sole survivor of the three brothers, returned to Lostock on his demobilization in February 1919.

Pozieres Memorial which bears the name of five Lostock boys.

The Lost Boys of Lostock

In Stanley Grove

No. 1: The three Corker brothers were quick to enlist at the Outbreak.

Most notably, Fred, aged 21, had left Brunner's with many of his mates, to join the 10th Cheshires, on the last day of August 1914. During his training at Codford St. Mary he seized the opportunity to take a specialist training course and, by the time the Cheshires sailed for France in September 1915, he was wearing, with pride, the 'exploding bomb' insignia of a first class practitioner with the hand-thrown Mills grenade. Fred, despite various trench raids, was to survive unscathed until July 1916 on the Somme where, on the evening of the 3rd, two days after the great battle had started, whilst relieving the Lancashire Fusiliers in the horrendously muddy front-line trenches near Aveluy Wood, he received a serious bullet wound to his thigh and was removed to base hospital for nearly four weeks. On July 31st, Fred, now fit, was drafted to the 1st Cheshires, whose numbers had been sadly depleted by the Somme fighting. Within two months, Fred was back in hospital. In the fighting at Morval (where his 1st Cheshires colleague was to win the Victoria Cross for killing three snipers and capturing over 100 Germans single-handedly), Fred received a gunshot wound to his left hand and a 'generous' dose of German gas. A few weeks in the No. 1 General Hospital at Rouen, followed

A newspaper from home.

by a period of convalescence back in Stanley Grove, soon had Fred back on his feet. He rejoined his battalion in the spring of 1917 and managed to survive until the Armistice with just one incident, in mid- 1918, winning a Military Medal for his bravery, when, in the words of his C.O. :

> When we were expecting an attack at dawn, he volunteered to reconnoitre the enemy's front line trenches, putting himself at considerable risk.

In December 1918, at Chester Castle, the home of the regiment, watched by his proud mum, Fred was presented with his medal by Lieutenant Colonel R.J. Cooke.

George and Joseph, Fred's brothers, both survived the War.

No. 3: Next door to the Corkers, at the home of his mother-in-law, Mrs Kelly, lived Arthur Furnival, his wife Anastasia and their three children. Arthur had enlisted on the first call, being assigned to 'A' company of the 12th Cheshires and spending much of his time in Salonika. In late August 1915, a letter confirmed that he would be arriving home early in September, for his first leave in nearly three years. As Arthur then appeared to have vanished, Anastasia, living in Crewe, wrote to the Military Paymaster at Shrewsbury seeking information on his whereabouts.

The following telegram was received on the 22nd October 1918:

> Regret to inform you, Private A. Furnival is reported dangerously ill at the No 1 Rest Camp Hospital, Cherbourg, France. If you would like to visit him, call for permit at Finsbury Court, Finsbury Pavement, bringing this telegram with you, or, if you are unable to bear the expense to London, take this telegram to the nearest Police Station.

Arthur had been taken ill on the voyage home and had been admitted to hospital suffering from leucocythaemia. Anastasia, now back in Lostock, quickly packed and left for Cherbourg, arriving at the hospital on the 29th, just two days before Arthur expired. She was probably the only Lostock wife able to attend her soldier-husband's funeral outside the home shores, as Arthur was buried with full military honours at Tourlaville Community Cemetery, some three miles from the centre of Cherbourg.

With a pension of 29s.7d per week, Anastasia and the children moved permanently to Crewe, where she was to marry a Mr. Leigh early in 1920.

The Lost Boys of Lostock

No. 19: John Tomlinson (known as Jack) was amongst the first of the Lostock Boys to attest, doing so on the 12th August 1914. On enlistment, he was initially assigned to the 2nd Dragoon Guards (The Buffs) but within six months he had transferred to the 8th Battalion of the Duke of Wellington's (West Riding) Regiment, which, by August 1915 was preparing to support the landings at Gallipoli.

His stay lasted short of two months, the events leading to his death being outlined in a letter received at 19 Stanley Grove later that year:

Pte.A.Furnival, Crp.J.Tomlinson

> Dear Mrs. Tomlinson,
> You will now know that your son, John, was killed while on outpost duty on the night of October 22nd. He had gone out with Sergeant Smith, from the same Company, in front of Jephson's Post, which position our Company was then occupying. Sergeant Smith returned alone and reported that Corporal Tomlinson had been killed by a bullet through his head. Sergeant Smith was very badly wounded in the leg and has since died of his wounds. Your son's body was found by the Royal Naval Air Service men a few days later and buried in front of our present line.
> There is no doubt that your son was killed instantly. Sergeant Smith reported to that effect. Both your son and Sergeant Smith volunteered and the praise and admiration of the whole Company is theirs for the dangerous work they undertook and, alas, gave up their lives for.
> I am one of the two officers left who did the landing here and you will quite understand what it has been for me to write so many letters like this; but, one and all, I feel very proud of our men and if I ever get home again, I hope I shall be able to visit and thank those North Country mothers, who have furnished a regiment such as I have had the honour to serve in.
>
> Cpt. S.E. Baker
> Suvla Bay, December 1915

John's grave was destroyed in subsequent fighting. He is commemorated, along with his companion on that fateful night, Fred Smith from Bradford, on the Helles Memorial, a 30 feet high obelisk, which stands at the very edge of the Gallipoli Peninsula, watching over the shipping sailing into the Dardanelles.

James, the elder brother, survived a lengthy period fighting in France, but was eventually seriously wounded and returned to Stanley Grove, permanently disabled.

Fate had still not washed its hands off the Tomlinsons as, a few days after the Armistice, John's mother and younger brother both died of influenza on the same day.

The Lost Boys of Lostock

No. 21: The stimulus for this account, Tommy Wrench, was the first of the Lostock boys to die whilst on military service but not in the line of battle. Joe Wrench, Tommy's Dad, was well respected as a railway shunter in the chemical works, where Tommy was to work in the short time he had between leaving school in 1910 and the Outbreak. In 1914 he enlisted and was assigned to the 14th Cheshires, a training battalion based in Rhyl, the recruits of which would be involved in the fighting only under exceptional circumstances.

Sadly, there is little information to be found on Tommy's very brief military career. It appears that he contracted an illness and died in hospital near Birkenhead in late March 1915.

He is buried in St. John's Churchyard, Lostock Gralam, and is commemorated on the War Memorials in both Lostock villages.

Tommy Wrench's headstone in St John's churchyard, with a stone recording his father's passing in 1913.

The old Slow and Easy on Manchester Road.

On Manchester Road

No. 33: Ernest Clarke had worked, both after school and on Saturdays, as an odd-job boy at Mr Rutter's Shoemaker's shop in Lostock Gralam. As he learned the business he realised that, despite the somewhat meagre pay, the job offered better prospects and more pleasant conditions than on offer at Brunner's. Thus, when young Ernie was offered a full-time job on leaving school in 1907, he was pleased to accept. The customers liked him, the work was 'clean' and the hours were regular. He spent many happy hours on the Alkali Club bowling green while in winter he moved inside and became a prizewinning billiard player at Lostock Club. On Sundays he could always be found in the choir stalls at St. John's Church.

On 1st September 1914, Mr Rutter would have been saddened to lose a thoroughly capable assistant of some ten years' standing, but not in the least surprised. Ever since

A horse picks its way past dugouts near the Front line.

the arrival of the Clarke family from Grimsby in 1902, Ernie had been popular in the community and, like so many of the village's young men, enlisted in the 10th Cheshires with his pals. However, whilst the majority of his mates became 'poor bloody infantry', Ernie's skills, acquired at Rutter's, meant he could work with leather and repair tack. No 'private's' rank for him – instead he became one of the 'horsemen', or saddlers. The 10th Cheshires had just over 950 men at full establishment but only eleven of them were classified as drivers for the horse-drawn transport, which consisted of 43 draught and pack animals, used for pulling the battalion's eleven carts – six loaded with ammunition, two with water and three General Service for tools and machine guns. The 10th Cheshires' first real battle experience was on the Somme in July 1916 when Ernie would have been fully involved in transporting the materials of war to the 'dumps' behind the front line. He supplied his battalion throughout the spring 1917 offensive and survived the great battle of the Messines Ridge.

Saddler E.Clarke

As the 10th Cheshires, part of the 25th Division, pushed forward, their Commanding Officer, Colonel A.C. Johnston, made a noteworthy entry in his diary as his men prepared for the attack on Pilkem Ridge, preparatory to the battle for Passchendaele:

> When we speak of reserves it is well to visualize what being in reserve in this type of warfare meant. As shelling and rain gradually churned up every yard of progress, the task of supplying the advanced troops with food, water, material for consolidation, and ammunition, assumed colossal proportions, and had to be borne by troops in so-called reserve. They themselves were not only liable to be called on to fight, and as often as not were so employed, to stem a retreat, to fill a gap, or to exploit a success, but were invariably required to take over the line and endure heavy punitive shelling, to allow the attacking troops to withdraw and recoup.
> So, when we read of such and such a Battalion being in reserve during an attack, we must not imagine them sitting behind a haystack on Salisbury Plain, but picture, rather, their ceaseless journeys in clinging and slippery mud, through mazes of communication trenches, crowded with wounded, and sometimes with beaten soldiers, carrying heavy loads, soaked to the skin, and enduring at every turn shelling purposely intended to hinder their progress.
> At other times, we can picture the reserves digging for dear life, in order to get some cover against the fury of bullet and shell with which the tenacious German was certain to support his inevitable counter-attack.
> This aspect of 'Reserves' is emphasized because, without their gallant labours, many a successful attack would have lost all its gains.

The Lost Boys of Lostock

Ernie and his fellow saddlers and pioneers had completed their duty and, on the 31st July 1917, were at rest, some distance from the front line, when simple devastation followed. His parents first received the news in a letter from the Battalion Chaplain:

> I am very grieved to tell you that your son, Saddler Clarke, was hit by a shell whilst in Camp this evening and brought to this dressing station, where he died shortly afterwards. He didn't suffer long, as he died soon after he was wounded. I knelt down by his side and offered prayers for him, but he was unconscious and unable to pray for himself . . . He has given his life for his country. May God cheer you and give you courage to bear this terrible blow. He will be buried here tomorrow.

A more personal letter followed describing events in much greater detail than the priest had managed:

> I am writing these few lines as I feel it a duty to do so and I can assure you it gives me great pain as I can hardly undertake such a terrible task. My heart failed me entirely when I read your beautiful letter to him and me knowing that he had been taken away from us. He has been my true chum and comrade all along and we were never apart.
>
> He met his death from a piece of shell and I was about ten yards from him. I was shaving and he was making some meal porridge for both of us as I had made the food the night before. He was bending down, along with six or seven of his comrades, when the shell came over. We were never expecting it, and everybody was quite happy and settled, and then this happened, and unfortunately my true chum met the hand of Fate.
>
> He was unconscious and within five minutes he was taken away in a Red Cross motor, and every day I have been waiting for news, expecting to hear that he was progressing, but, alas, the news was the reverse, and my nerves have been shattered by such a blow, and I have also lost my brother. He was miles behind the line, and the piece caught him in the thigh.
>
> Everyone mourns his loss, as he was so well respected, and he was a good soldier and comrade, and a chum unequalled. He will ever be remembered by all who knew him. He has been through many great dangers, and faced them bravely, always in my company, and he has done his duty well. I can assure you that he was a credit to his village.
>
> I wish to convey to you my deepest sympathy, and hope you will find some consolation in these few lines. May God help you to bear up in your bereavement, and if you wish to know anything more I shall feel it my duty to treat it as a great favour to give you the information required.
>
> Signed Private Alfred Cox

Ernie's life ended at the 69th Field Ambulance, which moved into a series of farm sheds on the road between Dickebus and Brandhoek, some four miles from Ypres. A cemetery was immediately established to deal with the dead from both the battles in the area and unsuccessful treatment in the Field Ambulances. Ernie was laid to rest on 1st September 1917 in the aptly named Huts. He was 24 years of age. In the local newspaper one year later, the 'In Memoriam' column contained the following under Ernest's name:-

> Farewell my dearest loved ones,
> A loving last farewell.
> The Lord has called me to Him
> And what he does is well.
> From Father, Mother, Bros and Sister

A War cemetery before C.W.G.C. developed them.

No. 113: The similarities in the lives and deaths of Samuel Forster and Ernest Clarke were remarkable. In age they were born within twelve months of each other; both had attended the local boys' school; they had taken employment in the retail market and, eventually, both were to give war service in unusual occupations; finally, having lived most of their lives within 200 yards of each other on the Manchester Road, they were to die within a few miles and 24 hours of each other.

Sam Forster had left school in 1908 to work in his dad's small greengrocery as an errand boy. Sadly the business had failed early in 1911 but young Sam had succeeded in gaining employment driving a horse-drawn delivery cart around the Northwich area. Such was his reputation that, when he decided to enlist in March 1915, he was given first class references by John Woodall, a prominent butcher, and Herbert Hopley, a well-known local grocer. Their supportive words enabled Sam to become a founder member of the 297th Company of the Army Service Corps as a horse driver. In May 1916, his Company had sailed from Southampton for the Western Front where, during the Battle of the Somme, the need for ambulance drivers had become so urgent that Sam and a number of his colleagues received a short training course allowing them to transfer to the mechanised lorries of the 138th Field Ambulance, essentially delivering severely wounded soldiers to the more advanced Casualty Clearing Stations.

138th Field Ambulance was part of the 41st Division which crossed to France in May 1916 and was involved in the fighting on the Somme, at Messines and outside Ypres. Sam had survived the fighting unmarked and provided sterling support moving the wounded across the battlefield. He was to be stricken by a quite unexpected enemy.

On 3rd September 1917, a telegram was received at Manchester Road bearing the dreadful news that Sam was dead. He had been admitted to the 37th Casualty Clearing Station suffering from abdominal pain. Appendicitis was diagnosed and an operation was performed on 22nd August. Sam appeared to be making a good recovery when, after five days, he collapsed. A second operation showed extensive peritonitis and Sam was declared dead at 8.30am on 30th August 1917. His remains were buried in the British Cemetery at Godewaersvelde, some 10 miles from Ypres – and just 6 miles from The Huts Cemetery where Ernest Clarke was to be buried the following day.

No. 65: Harry Bowyer had enjoyed a crowded life. At home, 65 Manchester Road, Mum, Martha, and Dad, John, had managed to produce four sons, three daughters and, sadly, two still-born children, between 1889 and 1902. Their three-bedroomed house coped with the crowd as John enjoyed relatively well paid employment at Brunner's as a chemical plumber; the family income was further boosted by his sons, James, the eldest, Harry (an apprentice joiner) and Douglas (a trainee grocer); all started work from 1903 onwards.

With the announcement of hostilities, Harry could not wait! News of the formation of a 'New Army' battalion of Cheshire men soon reached Lostock and he was on the first available bus to Chester where enlistment was underway in the Grandstand at the famous racecourse. By the 27th August, Harry had passed his medical and, despite having no uniform, no arms and no equipment, was one of a hundred men rushed to rendezvous with the 8th Battalion at Tidworth on Salisbury Plain. Gradually the men were trained (and equipped!) for war, and, in June 1915, they sailed from Avonmouth under the command of Lieut. Col. C.H.D. Willoughby, destined for Gallilopi, to serve alongside the Australian and New Zealand Light Horse Brigades. They won battle honours at Sari Bair and Scimitar Hill until they were ordered, in January 1916, to form the rear guard for the evacuation of part of the force from Suvla Bay. Within two months Harry and the 8th Cheshires landed in the inglorious chaos that was known as 'Messpot', or Mesopotamia to the politicians, who had allowed serious deterioration in Britain's control of the vital oil in the region. The Turks, in command of many of the major cities including Kut and Bagdhad, would have to be overcome – but the troops were suffering severely from the climate.

> [They] were worn out with diseases, dysentery, cholera and boils. Vegetables were not to be had. The temperature was 130 degrees in the tents . . . casualties . . . were very heavy. By the end of August the 8th Battalion mustered only 8 officers and 279 men (of the 750 men who would answer a full-strength call under ideal conditions).

Harry Bowyer was to finally meet his end in the trench fighting near Bagdhad. He had already survived a gunshot wound to his back some three months earlier in the initial advance on Kut, necessitating his two months of convalescence at Amara, but, despite the best efforts of the 47th Field Ambulance, a bullet to the head ended Harry's life. His grave was lost in later fighting and his name stands in perpetuity on the great Memorial at Basra to the 40,500 men who died in the fighting here between 1914 and 1921 and have no known grave.

No. 67: The Wood family, next-door neighbours to the Bowyers, had lived in Runcorn until father, James following the well-establish salt trail, had moved his family of eight to Northwich in 1900. With the supplements provided by the wages of John and James jr. the family, by 1911, were able to afford the rent on a bigger home in Lostock. James and his three sons all worked at Brunner's, whilst two of the three sisters had domestic jobs in the locality. The family was doing well but the autumn of 1914 was to witness a radical shift in their fortunes. In the flurry of enlistment, young Fred was first away and joined the 10th Cheshires on the last day in August. One day later 32-year-old John had enlisted too in the same battalion, but a different company. The brothers made good soldiers, John being promoted to Lance Corporal in May 1916 and Fred receiving his stripe just after the carnage of the Battle of The Somme. However, despite their remaining in close contact, their paths began to diverge, quite markedly, as the Somme battle ground to a halt in November.

As the Battalion fought doggedly to win ground north of Thiepval, news reached Lostock that Fred, having shown great courage in the hand-to-hand trench fighting, had been awarded the Military Medal 'for bravery in the field'. In his ten days of special leave that followed, Fred was fêted back home. He was the first local boy to be so rewarded and the community wished to demonstrate its admiration and congratulations. At a packed meeting in the local school, Fred was lauded by Parish Councillors W.D. Hesketh and J. Bladon (both of whom were to lose sons later in the war). His friends from Brunner's, team mates from both Lostock Gralam F.C. and the Alkali Bowling team, along with large numbers of villagers, had contributed to the purchase of a gold watch and chain. His award was gazetted in the third supplement to the London Gazette on 19th December, one week after Fred's arrival back at the Front.

The brothers survived the raids and trench fighting of Spring 1917; indeed, John received his only 'wounds' of the war during the period when he made lengthy visits to a Field Ambulance with influenza and dental problems. The Field Ambulance, No 77, was to prove highly significant in the life of the Wood family. After the great battle on the Messines Ridge, the 10th Cheshires were involved in the preparations for the planned attacks at Ypres. In mid-July, the brothers Wood were occupying trenches outside Pilckem, when Fred received a gunshot wound to the head, causing a cerebral hernia. He was rushed to the 77 Field Ambulance where he lingered for some ten days before finally expiring on 5th August 1917. Perhaps the death of Fred caused John to lose some of his love for the 10th Battalion as he sought, and was given, a transfer to the 9th Battalion, with whom he would see out the war.

Mendingham Military Cemetery, near Poperinge, in Belgium, is Fred's final resting place.

No. 72: Thomas and Harriet Jones had moved their family from the coal mines of Staffordshire to the chemical works at Lostock Gralam at the end of the nineteenth century. They had produced nine children along the way, three of whom, sadly, had died soon after their birth. By the early years of the new century the family were well established on Manchester Road, with Dad and the older boys working in the salt industry, being joined by youngest brother, William, on his leaving Lostock Boys School in 1907. Little else is recorded about William until he sailed for France in December 1915 as a Lance Corporal in the 10th Cheshires, achieving Corporal, then Acting Sergeant rank in early 1918. Despite his surviving the great battles of 1916 and 1917, William's life was to end in the fighting for the village of Kemmel on 26th April 1918.

> Shortly after dark on the 25th, the weather turned wet and by midnight the rain was falling in torrent . . . At 3am the Brigades advanced, soaked to the skin. The fog was thick . . . the attack could hardly have started in worse conditions.

As the men stumbled forward, with their way lit only by the flashes of heavy artillery and Very lights ripping into the sky, conditions worsened even more with the hail of machine gun bullets that whined their way across the morass. The 10th Cheshires' War Diary hinted at where the blame might lie for this latest failure:

> Considerable machine gun fire resisted our best efforts and our right flank, supposed to have been under French control, never attacked, only a rapidly thickening mist obscuring our weakness from the Germans – so our Brigade was forced to withdraw.

William Jones's fate was decided in the blackness. He simply disappeared, along with nearly a hundred of his mates, most of whom remained lost, in another futile venture. William has no known grave. His life and service are commemorated on the great memorial at Tyne Cot Cemetery. Nearly 12,000 bodies are buried there with a further 34,000 troops commemorated on the Wall of Remembrance. Tyne Cot is the biggest British and Commonwealth cemetery in the world.

> **No. 84:** Even now I can scarcely think of the scene that followed without trembling with horror . . . at 3.30am there was a deep muffled roar; the ground in front of where I stood rose up, as if some giant had wakened from his sleep and was bursting his way through the earth's crust and then I saw seven huge columns of smoke and flames shoot hundreds of feet into the air, while masses of clay and stones, tons in weight, were hurled about like pebbles. I never before realised what an earthquake was like, for not only did the ground quiver and shake, but actually rocked backwards and forwards, so that I kept on my feet with difficulty . . . hell itself seemed to have been let loose. With the roar of the mines came the deafening crash of our big guns .....never before, even

in this war, have so many batteries especially of heavy pieces been concentrated on one objective .....our shells fell like hailstones.

The author of these words, Jesuit Priest Father William Doyle, was Chaplain to the 16th Irish Division, who were waiting to attack Messines Ridge. What Father Doyle had witnessed was the result of eighteen months of effort by soldiers creating five miles of tunnels and laying over 600 tonnes of high explosives. On a seven-mile front under the Ridge, nineteen mines were exploded, killing over 10,000 German soldiers. Lloyd George heard the detonation, reputed to have been the loudest man-made explosion to that point in history, whilst reading in Downing Street. People in the streets of Dublin turned towards the muffled roar, not knowing that, for the first time, men from both sides of the Irish divide were attacking as comrades-in-arms.

In Lostock Gralam, perhaps the Gregory family, about to set about their morning duties, may have wondered what brother Charles was doing that day. Charles had tried to enlist at the Outbreak, but his youth was a hindrance until he succeeded in joining the Territorials in June 1916, leaving behind his job on Mr Wright's farm in Tabley. Within twelve months, the devastating losses of the first days of the Somme battles caused replacements, including Charles, to be rushed to the Front. He was to spend the remainder of his life in the 11th Battalion of the Cheshires. Both dedicated and popular, Charles survived the fighting on the Somme and, in March 1917, was promoted to Lance Corporal. Within two months he had his second stripe, and, with his platoon, prepared, with the Australian and New Zealand forces and the boys from the island of Ireland (being the 16th Irish and 36th Ulster divisions) for the great attack to be launched on the German occupied Messines Ridge in the early hours of the seventh of June 1917.

A letter from his platoon commander arrived at No. 84 on the fifteenth of June:

> I regret to inform you that your son, Corporal Charles Gregory, was killed whilst holding a newly captured trench against enemy counter-attack. He has been in the platoon for the last three months and was one of the best N.C.Os I ever had. He always did his duty and was always very cheerful about it. Please accept my heartfelt sympathy in your bereavement.
> 2nd Lt. T. Blackburn,
> 11th Cheshires

After the top had been blown off the Ridge, the allied troops quickly followed with a barrage of their own artillery and occupied the shattered German defences, all within three hours of the original explosion. Mustering the troops they had in reserve, the Germans counter-attacked immediately, the Ridge being a vital part of their defences around Ypres. Sadly, despite the Germans being repelled, Charles Gregory lost his life in that phase of the fighting. His body was lost in the heat of battle and his memory is commemorated just outside Ypres on the Menin Gate.

Crp.C. Gregory

An epilogue:
Of the 21 mines placed by the tunnellers, two remained undetonated. One had been discovered by German 'moles', whilst the other simply did not 'blow'. As time passed the land returned to its normal agricultural use, the whereabouts of the unexploded mine lost to memory. In July 1955 a severe thunderstorm broke over the old Messines battlefield. Lightning earthed right on the missing mine and in the massive explosion that followed there was to be one final casualty – a cow of the Dutch Blue breed. Charles, the cowman from Wright's farm at Tabley, would perhaps have smiled from his perpetual home.

Prayers before battle.

The Lost Boys of Lostock

A Truly 'Well-Known' Lostockian

IF ONE was to believe the local newspapers of the time, publishing their pages full of obituaries, one might feel that virtually every man who gave his life was 'well-known'. Undoubtedly many were, but the majority were simply 'well-known' to their families and friends.

One Lostockian who deserved the epithet above all others was George Henry Warburton of Manchester Road who was generally 'well-known' throughout Northwich, the Lostocks and even in the area surrounding those communities. George, having spent his time at Sir John Deane's Grammar School in Northwich, began his working life in 1896 as an assistant in his dad's butchers shops. During the next few years, he spent time working in Burgon's Grocery Store and Price's Stores in Hartford. The local newspaper, the Northwich Guardian, records in its report of July 1915:

> [He] was a man of many parts and nothing seemed to give him greater pleasure than to assist any cause that would benefit those with whom he was directly associate . . . he was one of the first to agitate for the formation of a branch of the Shop Assistants' Union . . . and for a while he acted as Chairman and, afterwards, Secretary..... During this time the (Union) had occasions to approach the Traders' Association Executive on the question of hours . . . and [He] proved himself an able advocate of the claims . . . and his position was always strengthened by the gentlemanly way in which he pleaded their cause.

His prowess as an organiser was further evidenced by his resurrection of the Northwich Wednesday Football team, his contribution to cricket in the town, his fine work as a lay preacher on the Northwich Wesleyan Church circuit and, not least, in the Northwich Brotherhood, where he was often praised for his positive contributions at meetings. The twenty-two local boys who had enlisted in the 3rd Rifle Brigade on 2nd September 1914 had embarked, as replacements, for France on 3rd May. George, already wearing his first promotional stripe, was with them. Within five days his short series of letters home began:

The Lost Boys of Lostock

To the Editor, Northwich Guardian
7th May 1915
From Guardian reports, Recruiting Meetings don't appear to have appealed to many of our young men. The war cannot last much longer. I do wish some of them could have seen our fighting men who have borne the brunt of the heavy winter's engagement, who have suffered frostbite and many other difficulties. A large number are so fearfully knocked about they will hardly be able to earn a living again. Surely this ought to be sufficient to make the laggards respond to the call so that it [the War] may soon be settled. This can only be done, I believe, by more men and the best we can absolutely give.

28th May 1915
I write to you hoping that all goes well with the shop assistants' campaign related to recruiting, of which I saw details in a recent issue of The Guardian which I receive weekly from a friend of mine and I might say it's always welcome.
During the past six days our Battalion has been in the firing line. We are about 150-200 yards away from the Germans and we have had some rather exciting moments. On one occasion they commenced to shell one of our working parties who were working by the ruins of a farmstead. One shell dropped almost amongst them. They scattered and no-one was wounded at all. The next one dropped about four yards away from where I was doing duty. It hit the top of our trench. Earth, sand and bricks fell in all directions. I bolted into my dug-out like a startled rabbit.
Between 5pm and 6pm we generally get a little 'special' treatment from the Germans after tea. They start pitching over rifle grenades and a thing which our chaps call either a 'cricket ball' or a 'football'. These are used to knock down our barriers to give us night work. Then they use shell lights to find out where our parties are working and use a machine gun on them.
I might say the Germans specialise in sniping. They are really adept in this line. The majority of their snipers use the rifle with a telescopic sight and it's a fact that if you show either a head, or half of one , for more than 4 seconds, all is up with you. The motto here is: - 'keep your head down.
We get very decent grub and plenty of it. It's been rather warm these past few days and we've been troubled with fleas. We have caught a few of 'these' enemies forming fours and doing platform drill using our shirts as the parade ground.
I must say that everybody is quite happy and expecting 'Fritz' will soon have had enough of it.
I must now close hoping that this will not be too long to enclose in your valuable paper.

The Lost Boys of Lostock

18th June 1915
Dear Editor,
It is with great pleasure that I write a few lines for the good old 'N.G.' which is sent to me regularly out here. I cannot tell you how much I appreciate reading about what our local boys are doing in different parts of the line and also all the interesting news about good old Northwich.

Just when I commenced writing this in our dug-out our assistant cook came with an issue of cigarettes, tobacco and dates which, you can bet, are extremely welcome. Just to show what a good chap he is last Sunday we had a 'regular burster' for dinner – stewed mutton, leeks and spuds. Not bad for the trenches is it? Everything was cooked to a turn and to think we fare like this within 200 yards of the Bosches. Our section cook, Darkie by name, is indeed a marvel at the stewpot. Goodness knows what we should do without him. In the morning he's up and gives us a cup of tea in our dug-out very often before the cock crows.

Dick Sweeney of Cross Street, Northwich, who was k.i.a. some time ago is buried about 50 yards behind our trench and one of the officers has promised to let me have a photograph of his grave for his sister. 'We have a nice lot of 'boys' in our section and every evening, before we retire, we have a bit of a singsong. I can assure you that it cheers us immensely, and we feel all the better for it.

Things have been fairly quiet for the last few days but you never know what to expect. We never leave anything to chance and are always ready for any emergency.

I had a letter from our people the other day in which they referred to Captain de Kroop's recent visit to Northwich and the appeal he made for recruits. Although differing from him in politics I say with all my heart 'Bravo Jersey!'

By the way we have a poet in our section and the other day, in his spare time, he came into my dug-out and scribbled out the following lines: -

>We are but little children meek
>We only get five francs per week
>The more we do, the more we may
>We hope they'll soon increase our pay.

25th June 1915
Dear Editor,
I am writing you a few lines again, this time from Belgium.
I have been simply astounded by the terrible havoc caused to this beautiful country by shell fire. For miles around as I gaze from this trench we are occupying, I cannot see a single building but what is in ruins. The most remarkable thing is the church property. The Germans seem to have made a special attack on them, but when you come to examine the church inside you find the image of Christ and the Blessed Virgin untouched and the same thing occurs when you find a crucifix in the house.

A few days ago I visited a farm and looked through the various rooms. All excepting one were in ruins and everything in that room excepting the piano was absolutely destroyed. I might say that the piano was in first class order and we might have had a little bit of a sing song only the enemy were a little bit too close and we should soon have been shelled out.

This past few days we have been continuously shelled by the Germans but they have not done any serious damage up to now. One or two men were wounded and I believe 2 men have been killed. On Tuesday they put 50 shells over in 30 minutes. These were 50 pounders but I am pleased to say no damage was done by shell fire at all. Their snipers keep very busy but I can assure you I don't give any chances by putting my head up.

I don't think I can say much more but I should like to make another appeal to all young men in Northwich and district who are still holding back to try and realise the seriousness of the situation and join the Army at once so that this war can be brought to a speedy conclusion.

In this last letter to the Guardian he gave a graphic and detailed description of the gallant British airmen in their actions above the trenches – and describes a major attack by the Rifle Brigade in which they captured 150 Germans and a large area of enemy trenches. The letter stated:

2nd July 1915
I should, in closing, like to appeal to all men at this time to put in every power they possess and work in some way to help the Government, and not to hinder them by strikes and so forth. It has been said that Germany kept peace for 26 years, but this was only a means to an end. All this time she had been preparing for war, and it appears to me the Germans have not overlooked any detail. So let us all unitedly, as a nation and a people, put first things first, and give of our spare time and our talents to help to overthrow the tyrant of Europe.

Crp.G. Warburton

George was, indeed, a prolific letter writer and, apart from his many friends, his younger sister, Mary, frequently received correspondence from him during his two months of service at the Front. After a two week period in Field Ambulance suffering from influenza, he wrote to Mary on July 15th 1915 as:

I have returned to the battalion in the trenches and you can now address all letters to me to the brigade, as above. It has been rotten as I have had no letters or anything from any one for nearly three weeks. All sent during that time have been forwarded all over everywhere and in the end I am not likely to get any of them. Well, I must not grumble. When you are in hospital you have to put up with those things. I am pleased to say no one has been killed in our section while I have been away. I have only been back about 48 hours and have not had a proper chance to look round, but will let you have a longer letter at the beginning of next week.

The very next day, the 16th, he wrote his last letter to a friend in the village of Hartford, near Northwich:

I was delighted to get your letter of the 12th, and I can assure you that I am always pleased to hear from my old district. I really get so many letters that my chief reason in writing to the 'Guardian' from time to time is to let friends know how things are, so that if I happen to have missed anyone they can see how I am faring out here. I have been away from the battalion for a fortnight as I have had a severe attack of influenza, but am glad to say I am now all right, and returned to duty on Tuesday last. We are at the moment in one of the hottest of all spots in the line, and we are due to come out of the trenches again on Sunday. I have been lucky in many ways while out here and I trust that as Providence has dealt so kindly with me up to now I may still have the same watchful eye overshadowing me until the end. I am writing this in my dug-out and all morning the Germans have been continually shelling us.

On 17th July 1915, George Warburton's pen was silenced forever. In the fighting at Hooge, near Ypres, he was to give his life for his country. One of his friends, Corporal William Kemp, wrote to Mary with:

Please excuse the liberty I am taking in writing to you, but by the time you receive this you will probably have heard from the War Office the sad news of your brother's death. I was with him to the last, and he left the enclosed packet in my charge until I had an opportunity of sending it to you.
As I am now home on a few days leave I am carrying out his wishes.
Your dear brother was shot through the lungs by shrapnel. He suffered no pain and I am sure you will take courage by knowing he died as a Christian and a soldier. He had no fear of death and was quite content to leave everything to Him who rules all. My mother and sisters join with me in expressing their deepest sympathy with you in your loss. I am sure he was a good brother, as he was a good chum. He was killed at Ypres and is buried behind the ruined town and his grave will be properly looked after while we remain here.

George's death had a more significant impact on the community than those of the later sacrifices as his passing came during the first full year of the War and before the local boys died in their droves on the Somme, at Passchendaele and, later, Ypres. The news reverberated around the towns, many tributes being paid in the churches, the sports clubs and in Union gatherings. In January 1916, what remained of George's personal effects, in accordance with his request in his soldier's will, were delivered to his sister. Essentially the packet contained the letters he had received from Mary and his many friends. Enclosed was his final, unposted letter to the newspaper, written on the day he died:

> We are situated at present in a terrifically hot quarter and yesterday our friends across the way shelled us continually the whole day, but don't for a minute think they had it all their own way, as we had a few of Lloyd George's 'specials' on hand, and we served them up quite hot, and, from what we have heard they are not very palatable when so served . . . whenever I have been in the line I have met N'wich men and they all seem merry and bright – good old 'Salts'.

Of the twenty two local boys who had enlisted in the 3rd Rifle Brigade in September 1914, George was to become the nineteenth casualty. He is buried at Potijze Burial Ground, near Ypres.

Army chaplain attending British graves.

The Lost of Lostock Green

A FAVOURITE Sunday walk for the Lostock Gralam residents in 1914 was along Station Road, heading south from St. John's Church, over the station bridge, through Lostock Hollows and up the hill to Beautybank Cottages. The road had now changed its name to Birches Lane and, after a short walk of no more than fifty yards [now occupied by the 60 mph dual carriageway of the A556] Robin Hood's Farm stood, and still stands, sentinel over the hamlet of Lostock Green. Today, the most prominent building in The Green is the Methodist Chapel, built in 1878 by the Hesketh family, prominent local millers. Outside is a small memorial bearing the names of just one Second World War casualty, Hubert Bell, and seven men who attended the Chapel before losing their lives in WW1. Of the seven, four were from Lostock Gralam and are considered elsewhere in this tome. Three lived in the hamlet – John Gleave and the Goodier brothers, William and Peter.

In 1901, John and Mary Gleave were living with their five sons, in Shipbrook Road, between Davenham and Rudheath; but the chance of a cottage at No. 42 Lostock Green offered the family growing room and John senior a shorter walk to his work at Brunner's. In 1905, the family moved and settled quickly into the small community of no more than thirty homesteads, mainly farms and their dependent cottages. John, the eldest boy, was given the job of leader of the one mile trek along Birches Lane into Station Road to the Lostock Gralam schools. Inevitably waiting for the Gleave troupe was Billy Goodier, John's newly-found best pal, with a clutch of younger Goodiers in his charge. The journey back to The Green sometimes dragged as the younger elements were tired and also wished either to do their almost ritualistic long-jumping over Wade Brook or to investigate the apple trees in a quiet corner of Springbank Farm. A quick reminder from John, almost imperceptibly the leader of the combined family force, of the proximity of the legendary giant, candle-bedecked pig of Lostock Hollows usually brought a fresh sense of purpose to the juvenile crocodile!

In 1907 Joe Gleave took the leaders baton when John joined his dad at Brunner's, working as general errand and tea boy in the first instance. However, his natural enthusiasm for life brought its own rewards and John was quickly to begin to climb the ladder. By 1914 he was already a foreman in the Works. As for many hundreds of thousands of young men, the war could hardly have come at a worse time. But it had to be dealt with and in late August, in response to Lord Kitchener's call for a third 100,000 volunteers, John finished his shift at Brunner's and, in the company of, amongst others, Jack Adamson, John Buckley, Archie MacDonald, Fred Wood and Billy Goodier, walked purposefully, if a little nervously, down the old Roman road to the recruiting office in Northwich, where they attested and were assigned to the 10th Battalion of the Cheshire Regiment. The example was set and, within days, two more of the Gleave brothers were in uniform; Joe in the Cheshires and Albert in the Royal Navy. Whilst the training and eventual embarkation for France could never be considered easy, having one's mates around from the Lostocks in general, and Brunner's in particular, made life almost acceptable. The Battalion, comprised of 800 absolutely raw 'civilians', without uniforms, weaponry or any experience, arrived at Codford St. Mary at the end of August. A young lieutenant was the sole officer, blessed with the task of bringing some kind of order to the chaos existing in the tented camp being swept by monsoon rains – without basic sanitary provision.

Lord Kitchener

Lieutenant Nares assembled the whole Battalion on the second morning, divided them into Companies and Platoons, then appointed temporary N.C.O.s using as his guide the hobbies and occupations the men had pursued in civilian life. Rankers from the various Boys' Organisations, Scouts, Boys Brigade etc. were quickly given promotions as were those men who had exercised some kind of authority in their civilian employment. To identify his N.C.O.s the lieutenant distributed strips of ribbon to be tied round the forearm in the stead of the traditional stripes. John was given a single ribbon, as a lance corporal, and took charge of a section of ten men, each one of them an old pal from Lostock. For a few days the blind followed the blind until at last a group of veterans arrived along with a number of very young Commissioned Officers, mostly straight from the Public Schools. Serious training began. As he was popular and commanded an easy respect, John Gleave kept his 'ribbon' and happily dealt with the teasing of his section when he paraded for the first time in uniform, sporting a genuine stripe.

The Battalion trained throughout 1915 under the gaze of Colonel F.V. Whittall, an officer who had retired from the Indian Army but had responded to the call for experience in the new emergency. After a final home leave in August, during which John felt slightly embarrassed when the congregation in the local Wesleyan Chapel prayed for the safe return of all their local sons and the minister insisted that John stood before the pulpit, the Battalion assembled near Aldershot and, on September 26th 1915, they crossed to France, just another piece in the jigsaw of Kitchener's New Army. For many of them it was to be a one way trip. Within three weeks of their arrival, the 10th Cheshires lost their first Lostock boy – and not to enemy action. Billy Goodier and his younger brother, Reggie [christened Raymond], missed The Green and their former existence. Letters from home only added to their nostalgia, especially as eighteen-year-old Peter had been given charge of a Sunday School Class at the Chapel, possibly as an inducement (which mum, Elizabeth, probably had a hand in to keep her youngest son away from thoughts of following his older brothers). In France the 10th Cheshires had been deeply involved in the battle near Ancre, in which they had successfully repulsed the counter-attacks by the Germans in some severe trench fighting, often hand-to-hand. Nearly 150 men had been wounded or killed but the Goodier boys had survived, along with their great pal, John Gleave, who had been promoted to Sergeant, both because of his efforts in the battle and because of the number of Senior N.C.O. casualties. On October 10th, the Battalion was given a well-deserved rest and marched back from the trenches in good spirits. They could now hope for a week or so in rest and recuperation, but normal duties still needed to be fulfilled. Billy was ordered to work on traffic control ensuring that the supply lorries and limbers enjoyed relatively unhindered progress past their tented camp to and from the front line trenches. In the dark, when much of the movement of food, water and ammunition was made, accidents were always one false step away.

At Lostock Green Elizabeth watched in real dread as her husband opened the letter:

> Dear Mrs. Goodier,
> It was with the deepest regret that I learned of the death of your son, William Goodier. He was knocked down by a motor lorry whilst on duty on the road and died two hours later.
> Though not in the firing line, he died doing his duty just as much as though he had been killed by enemy action. We shall miss him very much.

> Though quiet and unassuming, he was always cheerful and obliging, always ready to perform even the hardest task without a murmur of complaint. All of the officers – to whom he was very well known – join with me in expressing our deepest sympathy with you in your very sad bereavement.
>
> Yours sincerely,
2nd. Lt. C. John Watson
10th Cheshires

[Young 'Jack' Watson was himself to be wounded at Vimy Ridge in 1916, repatriated to recuperate and then attached as a full Lieutenant to the 8th Cheshires serving in Mesopotamia (our modern Iraq). He was killed on 26th January 1917, aged 24]

Two days after the arrival of Lieutenant Watson's letter, the postman called again. He carried a letter from Billy.

> Dear All,
> I hope this finds you as it leaves me, in good health and spirits. We have had a lively time recently but have now got some rest.
> I have left Reggie, who is well, and have got another job since I came out of the trenches – which is not quite so dangerous. Both of us are not going in the firing line for a while without there is a change in plans.
> Tell Dad to remember us to the other lads at Lostock for old times sake.
> Looking forward to seeing you one day soon.
>
> Your loving son, Billy
> PS. Tell our Peter to keep up the good work.

Pte. W.E. Goodier

As the family wept over his last words, Billy was being laid to his final rest in the Bailleul Communal Cemetery, a French town some 8 miles southwest of Ypres. 'Our Peter' was devastated. The big brother he had worshipped was lost while he was teaching in the calm of the Methodist Sunday School. Over the next few days, Peter said very little. He felt rather detached from the family's grief, knowing that he had a big decision to make that would not lessen his mother's grief. On his daily walk to and from his employment at the Ammonia Soda Works in nearby Plumley, he pondered. His objective was simple – to seek revenge for Billy. But this was no time to discuss his intentions at home. Thus, one afternoon soon after Christmas, Peter went to the recruiting office in Northwich and asked for assignment to the Regiment needing recruits most immediately. At Hawthorn Cottages, the news was less than well received. Peter was to join the Duke of Wellingtons [West Riding] Regiment and would be leaving within days.

In the Spring news came that Reggie had been wounded but was in fair shape. He had spent some time in a French hospital but was now about to return to the trenches. The pressure on the Goodier family was palpable. William senior at least had his work as a carter for the Midland Lines to occupy him during the day but Elizabeth depended more than ever on her daughters for comfort. In the summer of 1916, the 10th Cheshires were decimated in an attack on Bazentin in the days following the Big Push of July 1st on the Somme. In two days 400 men were either killed, wounded or missing from that one Battalion, Reggie Goodier again suffering severe wounds, which this time brought his war to an end. After a spell in hospital, he returned to The Green where all was not as he might have expected. His mother had been for some time, in failing health, no doubt her

The Lostock Green memorial.

problems exacerbated by the tribulations in battle of her sons. On 5th January 1917 Elizabeth died and was buried in St. John's churchyard.

The Goodier family were soon to share in a new sadness. In mid-February 1917, the 10th Cheshires were involved in a major raid on the German trenches in the Ploegsteert sector, about eight miles south of Ypres town centre. Units which were in need of rest were normally sent to this 'quiet' sector to recover after hard fighting. However, trench fighting on a local scale was carried on by both sides. On one such raid, misguidedly expecting their artillery to have shattered the German wire defences, 200 men of the 10th Cheshires were ordered into a night attack. Carnage followed as the machine gunners trapped the men on the largely uncut barbed wire. John Gleave was seriously wounded in the raid but managed to regain his own trench. He was rushed to a dressing station where staff quickly realised his injuries were beyond their scope. Along with a large number of other seriously wounded, he was transported from the battlefield to a Field Hospital and from there, by train, to a hospital in Boulogne. Although John fought them with his usual enthusiasm, he succumbed to his wounds on 6th March 1917. He is one of over 5,500 Commonwealth soldiers buried in the Boulogne Eastern Cemetery. The Gleaves, like the Goodier family, had lost their oldest child, yet both families faced a future in which more sacrifices might be demanded.

The Duke of Wellington's [West Riding] Regiment, 9th Battalion was battle-hardened by the time Peter Goodier joined them in a new draft from their training battalion in the autumn of 1917. They had fought, and given excellent account of themselves, in most of the major battles since their arrival in France as part of Kitchener's second 100,000 men (or 'K2') in July 1915, but losses had been heavy on the Somme, at Arras and at Ypres. Peter had survived fierce fighting at the second battle of Passchendaele in late October and then in the great German offensive of 1918, known as the Kaiser's Battle. By the late summer, Peter and his fellow 9th 'Duke's' were fighting alongside nine Divisions of Australians and Canadians outside Amiens in a battle which was to see the beginning of the end for the German army, which suffered nearly four times the casualties of the Allied force. Nearly 100,000 men were wounded, killed or missing in a three-day period. On 1st September 1918 Peter's luck ran out. Attacking trenches outside Bapaume, he received a fatal bullet wound and, the next day, was given a battlefield grave. As this was lost in subsequent artillery fire, Peter is now remembered on the Vis-en-Artois Memorial, along with the names of nearly 10,000 other Commonwealth soldiers who died in the last three months of the War in that region and have no known grave.

The Green had lost three of its sons.

The Lost Boys of Lostock

The First of the Many ... and the Last

THE FIRST

A somewhat chequered childhood caused by the early death of his father, before Sam Whittaker had achieved his tenth birthday, meant that most of his formative years were spent living with the family of his mother's brother, Henry Eyres, in Griffiths Lane.

After a relatively undistinguished school career, Sam was pleased to find work as a labourer on Crown Farm in Peover. However, the life described to him by his cousin, George Eyres, then a serving soldier, seemed to offer more than the hard life of a farm labourer. Thus, in October 1903, Sam walked to Knutsford Recruiting Office and joined the Cheshire Regiment. After two years of training, the second battalion set sail for garrison duties in India, where he was to enjoy life so much that he extended his original three-year contract to eight. His records indicate that, apart from a couple of unscheduled leaves of absence and an unpleasant 'illness', picked up from a period of dalliance with a local lady of the night, Sam saw out the next six years in relative comfort.

English soldiers near Mons.

The Lost Boys of Lostock

When his time expired, he returned to Lostock in November 1911 and secured employment at Brunner's, where he remained until the Outbreak, whereupon, as a reservist, he was mobilized on the 5th August, probably the first non-serving Lostockian to answer the call. As his old battalion was just making plans to leave India, Sam was assigned, with immediate effect, to the 1st Battalion, who, because of the crisis developing on the European mainland, were immediately entrained from their camp at Londonderry, where they had been monitoring the unrest in Northern Ireland, for the S.S. Massilla in Belfast Docks. They disembarked at Le Havre on that day, 16th August 1914. Within eight days, Sam and the vast majority of his comrades were to become casualties in the carnage around Mons, the town in Belgium near the French border. Although starting the 24th August in reserve and only moving into the front line, near the village of Audregnies, at about 9.30am with some 25 officers and 952 other ranks, by the 9.00pm roll call, after a day of savage fighting against vastly superior numbers, the 1st Cheshires suffered over 75% casualties, being left with just 7 officers and under 200 men. Sam Whittaker was one of the many missing.

Pte.S. Whittaker

There was to be no early closure for his mum, Elizabeth, and the Eyres family. Sam, like so many of his mates, was simply 'missing'. The family waited, clutching the hope that, like a considerable number of the men of Mons, he had become a prisoner. Throughout the autumn and winter the family waited. News of the Cheshires was brought from the Front by the wounded. Perhaps the story of the Angels of Mons might have given Elizabeth renewed hope, but winter 1915 became spring and still Sam's disappearance remained unexplained. Letters were sent from Griffiths Lane both to the local newspaper and, even more hopefully, the War Office, but no explanations were forthcoming. It

Life in the Trenches.

was not until the spring of 1916 that Henry received a reply to his letter of Christmas 1915 when he had virtually begged the War Office for information. 'Sam is missing, presumed killed, and has been so since August 24th the previous year at Audregnies.'

Over 4,000 men of the British Expeditionary Force were killed in the first ten weeks of the war, most of them regular soldiers, like Sam, who were just doing their job. Large numbers of them are commemorated on the memorial at La Ferte-sous-Jouarre, in the Seine-et-Marie region. Sam's remains were lost for all eternity but his sole claim to everlasting fame prevails – he was the first of Lostock Gralam to die in the war.

THE LAST
The last Lostockian to be killed in battle was Clarence Wilfred Jones, oldest son of a long-established village family. He had attended the local boys' school until he took an apprenticeship. His father, Arthur, a building inspector at the Northwich Railway Station, had determined that work at Brunner's offered fewer opportunities than those afforded by George Pemberton's joinery business in Knutsford. Clarence prospered and, in 1910, he was appointed as a time-served joiner. However, like so many men of his generation, Clarence answered the call to arms early and, in November 1914, he enlisted in the 21st battalion of the Manchester Regiment commonly known as the 6th Pals. During his training he transferred to the South Lancashire Regiment with whom he crossed to France in November 1915, leaving the comforts of Lostock behind but with the full support of his local Wesleyan Church in whose choir he had figured prominently.

Pte.C.W. Jones

Clarence survived the bloodshed of 1916 and 1917 but would have been horrified at the deaths, in a three-day period in October 1917, of his cousins, John Faulkner of Lostock, Sam Burgess and Tom Gilbert of Knutsford. In February 1918, when his South Lancs battalion was disbanded, Clarence elected to join the 19th Lancashire Fusiliers, originally the 3rd Salford Pals and part of the 49th (West Riding) Division. By early October 1918, the war had turned for the last time with the German army in full retreat but of sufficient strength to put serious obstacles in the path of pursuing Allied forces. One such obstacle proved to be the village of Haspres, adjoining the River Selle. Alongside two battalions from the York and Lancasters, the 19th Lancs. Fusiliers attacked at 8.00am on October 13th. They were met by a storm of German machine gunfire, supported by a heavy artillery bombardment. On that day, one hundred and thirty seven British troops lost their lives.

There are two military cemeteries in the countryside by Haspres – Coppice Cemetery, where are buried fifty Lancashire Fusiliers and York Cemetery, where lie over one hundred York and Lancs men and just two Fusiliers. One of these is 26 year old Clarence.

And Finally ....
Twenty three year old Manchester Road resident, Lieutenant Edward Webster, killed in a motoring accident in Mesopotamia, is buried in Haidar Pasha Cemetery in the suburbs of Istanbul. He was the last Lostock man to be killed on active service on 12th September 1920.

In January of that year, Thomas Hall (q.v.) died in a London hospital. Two men, however, had died days short of the Armistice – Thomas Snelson (q.v.) of influenza in Limerick on 2nd November 1918 and Arthur Furnival (q.v.) who died in hospital in Cherbourg on the last day of October.

Manchester Road, Lostock Gralam.

They Also Served

Fred Cawley: A regular soldier before the Outbreak, Fred had purchased his release in 1913. However, in late August 1914 he answered the call and joined the 2nd Cheshires. Experienced, Fred was sent to the Front on 3rd January 1915, where he was shot in the head within four months, in the fighting near Hill 60 at Ypres. Fred's wound was so severe that he underwent a trepanning operation in a French hospital before being evacuated to England to convalesce. His fitness for soldiering being over, Fred spent the rest of the war on munitions work at Brunner's

Albert Rainford: One of the many victims of the Battle of the Somme in 1916 was Albert Rainford, who had joined the 10th Cheshires with a large number of his Brunner mates, in late August 1914.

Albert was wounded outside the Bazentin village on the 15th July. A later Medical Board report read:

> In an attack on the German trenches, he was hit by a machine gun bullet which . . . entered his forearm, passed through the joint and fractured the external condyle of the humerus . . . The arm can only be held at a right angle and the extension of the forearm is lost.

After spending over twelve months in a military hospital and in recuperation, a medical board declared him unfit to serve and he was discharged in September 1917. Albert's reprieve was short lived as he was to die from septic pneumonia in February 1919. His family remembered his passing by recording his name in the Roll of Honour for the war dead in the local newspaper. Albert is buried in St. John's churchyard.

Vere Jones: William and Robert Jones survived the war relatively unscathed, but their youngest brother, Vere, was to carry his burden until his death. As a member of the 8th Cheshires, Vere had suffered the heat and disease in Mesopotamia until, in late 1916, a sniper's bullet left him totally blind and with an impaired memory. On his return to Lostock after months of hospitalization, his colleagues at Ammonia Soda held a benefit

*Wounded British arriving by ambulance at
Amiens hospital, early 1915.*

concert for him in their overcrowded works' canteen, which raised £45.00 for Vere. A variety of artistes gave their services free, including Mr. B. Soward, who sang the unfortunately titled 'Total Eclipse'. Vere died aged 75 in 1966 and is buried in St. John's churchyard.

George Bell Heath: Seriously wounded in the fighting on the Somme, he spent over one year in the War Hospital in Bradford where his doctors recorded: 'Loss of much-comminuted bone from the head of his humerus. His arm is still very stiff at the elbow and shoulder.' So severe were his wounds that he was discharged from the 10th Cheshires and was permanently excluded from all liability to Medical Re-examination on 31st August 1917.

William Dalton: William was discharged from the Cheshires in May 1917, having spent some six months in the 2nd Western Military Hospital in Manchester recovering from gunshot wounds to his forehead, wrist and right leg in the 1916 fighting on the Somme.

Elias Arthur Green: Fighting with the 11th Cheshires in the early days of the Battle of the Somme, Elias received a very severe gunshot wound to his upper jaw. By the 22nd July he was back in England at the Cambridge Hospital, Aldershot where he was to remain for nearly twelve months. He was discharged from the army in July 1917, pensioned to the tune of 6/3d. weekly for twelve months and granted permanent exemption from liability to Medical Re-examination.

Sidney Barber: Sidney had joined the rush to enlist in the 10th Cheshires in August 1914 and had survived unscathed until he was struck by a bullet at Messines in June 1917. Worse was to follow. In August of that year he was blown up by German artillery fire and lost his left leg. A crowded Lostock Pavilion held a benefit concert for him, in January 1918, whilst he was recovering in Alder Hey Military Orthopaedic Hospital.

George and Arthur Cross: They were two of the five, fighting Cross brothers. In 1915 George was severely gassed outside Ypres, leading to his discharge from the army in August of that year. Arthur, with the Manchesters, had received a severe gunshot wound to his skull on the Somme and, in December 1916, was also discharged.

William Leicester: His home in Moss Lane and Leach's farm in Allostock would have seemed a million miles away when William Leicester and his 10th Cheshire pals joined the front line trenches at Ovillers on 2nd July 1916, the second day of the Battle of the Somme. The fighting was savage, marked by intensive artillery fire. The battalion suffered over 400 casualties in a ten day period. William suffered gunshot wounds to his arm and right leg necessitating his repatriation to a London hospital where his leg was amputated above his knee. After months in hospital he returned to Lostock supported by a pension for life of 27/6d per week.

The Silver War Badge (S.W.B.)
During the Great War it was not unusual for young women to hand the white feathers of cowardice to apparently able-bodied young men, who walked the streets in civilian clothes. Frequently, young men who had 'done their bit' but were too damaged to return to the Front, were embarrassed by these female zealots. Thus, from September 1916, during the bloodbath on the Somme, the War Office issued the S.W.B. known colloquially as the Silver Wound Badge.

The Lost Boys of Lostock

Many of the men of Lostock are on the S.W.B. list including:
William Dodd, High Bank Farm, 1/5th Cheshires
John Earle, 'Avondale', Manchester Road, Welsh Regiment
Benjamin Bates, Brook Street, 3rd Cheshires
Harry Mather, Manchester Road, Machine Gun Company
Albert Rainford, Manchester Road, 10th Cheshires
John Rainford, Manchester Road, 2nd Cheshires
Samuel Hitchen, Renshaw Street, 2nd Cheshires
Frank Goulding, School Lane, 10th Cheshires
Vere Jones, Manchester Road, 8th Cheshires
George Heath, Manchester Road, 10th Cheshires
William Dalton, Manchester Road, 10th Cheshires
Elias Arthur Green, Austen Street, 11th Cheshires
Sydney Barber, Boundary Street, 10th Cheshires
George Cross, Renshaw Street, 3rd Rifle Brigade
Arthur Cross, Renshaw Street, 6th Manchesters
William Leicester, Moss Lane, 10th Cheshires
John Southern, Arthur Street, 3rd Cheshires

Recruiting more men for the Front.

The Lost Boys of Lostock

Letters from Sam Hitchen

AMONGST all the letter writers Sam Hitchen of Renshaw Street produced some of the most graphic epistles received in Lostock – certainly during the early part of the war. Sam was a time-served 'terrier' by 1912 but, on 1st September 1914, he re-enlisted in the Cheshires and, within a few months, sailed for France with the 2nd Battalion. His letters home started almost immediately.

1) Over the Top

I have just enough time to tell you a little of my experiences since I came out to the Front. My first experience of going into action is one that will require some forgetting. We had orders to stand to about three o'clock in the morning and we marched off at four. We were given to understand that the Germans were making a final effort to break through our lines. We quite expected to have a good reception before we got where we wanted, as going into action in the daytime and going to the firing line at night is a bit different. Our expectations were realised sooner than we were aware of. The first intimation we had from the Germans was a gas shell or two. I was fortunate I think, to be about 80 yards behind the first shell, but it did not stop me from getting my eyes full and a small quantity got down my throat. I soon had my respirator round my mouth and nose, but I could not bear my eyes open for about ten minutes or more. The gas they use is terrible stuff, but the brutes thought wrong if they imagined that would make us take the right about. We had orders that we were wanted in the firing line, and that was enough for us. Our sergeant deserves some credit. Some of our boys with their officers soon found another way across some open fields before the Germans saw them, but just as our platoon was about to make a dash across the same fields they must have seen some of us as they began sending shrapnel and it rained shells. Our platoon lay behind a little ridge when our sergeant jumped up and shouted, "Come on boys!" That did it, for we jumped like one man.

I need to think that I could get along the wing when I played with Witton Albion Reserve and Lostock Gralam. We had orders to discard our packs before we made a dash for it, but without them we had plenty to carry, as we had lead pills for the Germans. We each carried two bandoliers extra besides our pouchful. If you had seen me make a bee line for the reserve trenches you would have thought it was Grocott. All I thought about was getting there. In the open we would have been simply cut to pieces. Nothing could live anywhere near the place we cut across. Our brave sergeant was wounded whilst going across, in fact we lost a good many plucky fellows. The trenches we got in. I made a dive for them and as the Germans continued to send 'whizz-bangs', 'coal-boxes' and 'Jack Johnsons', we stayed in them for a few hours. It would have been madness to even turn in them and as they were old trenches and no more than two feet six inches deep by about 15 inches across I had cramp in both my legs and back with being in one position for so long, as I could not turn without raising myself over the top, and if I had done so I would not have been here now to tell this tale. Some of the shells which the Germans send, what we call 'whizz-bangs', just skim the top of the trenches. We cannot hear them until they pass but they make a terrible row when they explode and nearly bury us with sand. I had as much sand down my neck as I think would fill a small bag.

One of our corporals, two away from me, just put his hand on the side of the trench to ease his position, and he had the end of his first finger taken clean away. The order came to us after we had been crouched up for about four hours to make for the fire trench. After going I should think about two miles down, we had to cross some open ground, and the Germans and the Germans caught us again with their shells. The only thing which troubled us we could not have our own back then, but that came later.

We had our own back with interest and compound interest at that. We got nearer and nearer to our goal, although it cost us some brave comrades. The last trench we had to go through was nearly up to our thighs in water and extremely narrow. We had another open field or two to cross, and still the German gunners gave us no peace. Shells were dropping like hailstones. We swore we would make them pay, and dearly at that, when we got near them. I should say more than half our comrades were killed and wounded. The sights I saw that day will, I think, cling to my mind so long as my life lasts, although I may try to forget them.

About two hundred yards from our destination was the hottest of the lot. I was lying prone on the ground when there was a rain of lead, old pieces of pig iron ore and all sorts of scrap iron. I think the women of Germany will have to iron their linen with something else because flat irons were flying about like flies. Pieces of shells were screaming all about me, and I do think some guardian angel must have been watching over me that day. I raised my head and asked if anyone had seen my chum, Sammy Jackson, and strange to say, Sammy answered himself. He was struggling up the incline with, I should think, three boxes of ammunition for his machine gun. He was carrying his own share and another chap's, and sweat was streaming down his face. When he replied to me I said, "What ho Sam! What are you doing up there?" I made sure he had gone under but when he answered I was greatly relieved. "Come down here," he said, "and give a hand with this lot." I had some trouble to get where I did, and possibly if I had got up I might have had a sniper's bullet, and pretty quick. It is not very often they miss. Snipers get in old barns, up trees, and in various hiding places. When we met I thought we would be able to have a chat, but the order came to advance, and again we had to face a withering shell fire. It tore gaps through us, but we were Cheshire boys, and belonged to a regiment that requires some beating out there. Times without number has our regiment been praised for its gallant deeds. Although it is not to the fore in the papers, all are brave fellows.

The last hundred yards we did in extended order, and that sort of advancing fairly beat the German gunners. They cannot understand the British form of advancing. The German snipers then got busy, and a fellow in front of me being hit in the neck was killed outright. Another chap behind got hit in the chest, and, dear mother, I think I am the luckiest chap who comes from Lostock. My comrades were dropping all around me and never a scratch did I receive. After getting in the trench and a short rest, we began to get ready to make things hum for Van Kluck's fanatics. Everything was ready in double quick time. We had orders to fix bayonets and await the order to advance. We were at the end of a small wood with the Germans at the other. About two o'clock in the morning the order came for us to advance, but the Germans heard us coming somehow, and I believe each of them had a machine gun. I am sure they thought the whole British army was after them that day, the row we kicked up, but it was only the Cheshire boys with their blood up. I am proud to belong to the Cheshire Regiment. Our officers are as brave as lions, and a word from them is enough for us. After the charge I was one of the lucky fellows out of a small batch to creep in the trench. I was feeling rather done up, but we achieved what was wanted of us. We were relieved the next night by a regiment from the North, and a day or two afterwards we were congratulated on our work, but we left many a brave Britisher behind, although they had not died in vain. Two of my chums were amongst those who fell that day. The Germans must have lost a great many men more than us. If it was not for their cowardly and underhand work Belgium would have been clear of their fiendish presence long ago. Thomas Barton, Harry Hines, McCulloch and another friend of mine, Sammy Jackson, are all in the pink and we are all good chums. Sammy Jackson, I heard afterwards, had been gassed, and he was in hospital four days. He is a machine gunner, and I may say full of fun when we are having a rest.

2) Dreadful Sights

Tell Joe to send good m.organ so that I can play it when we come out of the trenches. Some of the Lostock boys had it extremely hard last winter, but I have taken part in the battle for Y-s (Ypres) and, being in battle, and being in the trenches, is very different. We started out with 500 men and came back with 175 so you can tell what I've gone through.

Shells were dropping every foot, never mind yards. When one dropped among us it was generally about twelve men it put out.

There is not a man breathing who can stick the sight I saw that day without being awe struck. Ever since we came out here we have heard the sound of guns night and day. The last night or two in the trenches were rotten. When we got close to, we could smell nothing but dead men. I am as well as ever I was, considering all things. It needs a chap with nerves to stick the horrible sights.

On Whit Mon. we got the order to fix bayonets and advance. I seemed to ab-

solutely care for nothing and hardly knew where I was for a while.
I have just been paid 10f. which is 8/4d in English money, and went to a farm to buy some bread. Some women came running up and said some German had blown their house up. It is pitiable to see the houses and towns with nobody in them. They are nothing but ruins. I have seen little girls and very old women with nowhere to go. The Germans will pay dearly for their cowardly work. While I am writing the Germans are shelling a village about 1 mile away. They have set it on fire. It's impossible to imagine what it's like here unless you saw it.

3) A German Gift
Thank Joe for the m. organ which I play whenever I can . . . . .the bombing is as bad as ever but now the Canadians have relieved us. I have never seen bigger chaps in my life!! They began singing as soon as they entered the trenches, 'Sing us a song of Bonnie Scotland'. We told them that Lostock was in England but it made no difference!
One night a German shouted across to ask if there was anybody from Cheshire in our trench. Some of the lads shouted "Yes!" and the German shouted back "Well, here's some Cheshire Cheese!" and he threw a bomb over, "Share that between you!" It wounded one or two of our chaps but I don't think the German who threw it will ever throw another!
We've asked them to come out into the open to fight but they refused so we're just going to blow them out lock, stock and barrel.

4) A Wounded Pal
Since my last letter I have been in two bayonet charges and the sights were horrible. We lost a lot of our boys. Some of the Prussian Guards stood right on top of their sandbags and threw bombs, fired rifles grenades and all sorts of explosives, but I have come through again.
The people of England do not realise what it is like over here. Three rows of Prussian Guards were waiting for us when we made the charge. I helped one of our poor lads, who was shot through the chest twice. I must have carried him for two miles to an old quarry from which we had previously driven the Germans.

Soon after this final letter, sent in mid-October 1915, Sam and the 2nd Cheshires were sent to Salonika to support the Serbian army. The 2nd Cheshires were stationed in the Struma Valley, rated as one of the unhealthiest places on the planet. Within a very short time the local mosquito population had done its work – 700 of the Battalion's number had been hospitalized and only 300 of them would return to the trenches.

Sam Hitchen was repatriated and ended the war working in Yarwood's ship building yard in Northwich. He was awarded the Silver War Badge because of his chronic malaria.

The Lostock Fallen Killed in Action by Regiment

1st Cheshires
Blain C.V.
Deakin S.
Deakin W.H.
Miller He.
Whittaker S.
1/5th Cheshires
Ashley Ed.
Deakin J.W.
Postles H.
2nd Cheshires
Sherlock W.
3rd Cheshires
Garner J.
8th Cheshires
Bowyer H.
Carter C.
10th Cheshires
Adamson J.
Ainsworth W.J.
Buckley J.W.
Clarke E.
Foxley J.
Gleave J.H.
Goodier W.E.
Hesketh W.
Hickson T.
Hulme J.
Jones W.
Kelly J.G.
Kettle A.
MacDonald A.
Southern G.

Southern W.
Timmis F.
Wood F.
11th Cheshires
Goulding G.
Gregory C.
Pickering W.
12th Cheshires
Connolly J.W.
Connolly T.H.
Furnival A.
Webster E.
14th Cheshires
Wrench T.H.
15th Cheshires
Bladon J.
16th Cheshires
Riley G.
18th Kings Liverpool
Baddeley H.S.
Royal Engineers
Hunt R.
2/9th Manchester
Faulkner J.T.
17th Manchester
Snelson G.
2/6th Royal Warwicks.
Johnson H.
D. of W. (W.R.Regt)
Goodier P.L.
Tomlinson J.
7th Norfolks
Miller Ha.

1/4th South Lancs.
Connolly L.
1/5th South Lancs.
Pickering H.E.
6th South Lancs.
Bramhall J.
Lancs. Fusiliers
Jones C.W.
Marlow G.
Army Service Corps.
Forster S.
Royal Field Artillery
Foxley V.A.
Northumberland Fusils.
Hall T.
7th Queens Own
Thompson J.
2nd Sth Wales Borderers
Walsh R.
Royal Welsh Fusils.
Snelson T.
9th Welsh
Smith J.
2nd Rifle Brigade
Southern T.
3rd Rifle Brigade
Warburton G.H.
Canadian Infantry
Davenport T.
Drinkwater W.
Johnson W.

Killed in Action by Street

MANCHESTER ROAD	No.
Ashley Ed.	
Bowyer H.	65
Clarke E.	33
Forster S.	113
Gregory C.	84
Hesketh W.	
Jones W.	72
Marlow G.	30
Pickering H.E.	119
Pickering W.	119
Warburton G.	67
Webster E.	83
Wood F.	67

SCHOOL LANE
Baddeley H.	17
Goulding G.	3
Hulme J.	45
Hunt R.	57
Riley G.	25
Southern G.	8
Southern T.	8

BROOK STREET
Ainsworth W.J.	8
Connolly L.	16
Connolly J.W.	16
Connolly T.	16

ANN STREET
Deakin S.
Deakin W.

BOUNDARY STREET
Blain C.V.	8
Buckley J.W.	22
Faulkner J.T.	23
Johnson H.	26
MacDonald A.	25
Postles H.	28

STATION ROAD
Bladon J.	
Carter C.	1
Foxley J.	2
Foxley V.A.	2
Kettle A.	52
Miller Ha.	18
Miller He.	18
Snelson G.	17
Snelson T.	17
Timmis F.	3

LOSTOCK GREEN
Gleave J.H.	42
Goodier P.L.	22
Goodier W.E.	22

RENSHAW STREET
Adamson J.	4
Hickson T.	7
Kelly J.G.	22
Thompson J.	18
Walsh R.	2

VICTORIA STREET
Smith J.

SMITHY LANE
Sherlock W.	7

OLD HALL LANE
Wrench T.H.	2

FITTON STREET
Bramhall J.	6

HEWITT STREET
Deakin J.W.	21

STANLEY GROVE
Furnival A.	3
Tomlinson J.	19

HERBERT STREET
Garner J.	6
Hall T.	1

HALL LANE
Jones C.W.	4

ARTHUR STREET
Southern W.	14

GRIFFITHS LANE
Whittaker S.	2

HOMES IN CANADA
Davenport T.
Drinkwater W.
Johnson W.

Where They Lie

MENIN GATE
Gregory C. (11th C)
Drinkwater W. (Canada)
Sherlock W. (2nd C)
VIMY MEM.
Davenport T. (Canada)
Gregory C. (11th C)
POZIERES
Bladon J. (15th C.)
Goulding G. (11th C)
Johnson H. (2/6 R.War.)
Snelson G. (17th M/c)
Thompson J. (7th Q.O.)
TYNE COTT.
Faulkner J. (2/9th M/c)
Jones W. (10th C)
Timmis F. (10th C)
Walsh R. (2nd S.W.B.)
MENDINGHAM
Wood F. (10th C)
LOOS MEM.
Foxley J. (10th C)
MacDonald A. (10th C)
BASRA MEM.
Bowyer H. (8th C)
Carter C. (8th C)
THIEPVAL MEM.
Adamson J. (10th C)
Buckley J. (10th C)
Southern G. (10th C)
BAILLEUL
Goodier W. (10th C)
Hesketh W. (10th C)
FLATIRON COPSE
Blain C.V. (1st C)
LE TOURET MEM.
Deakin S. (1st C)

ARRAS MEM.
Ashley Ed. (1/5 C)
Kelly J. (10th C)
SPOILBANK
Deakin W.H. (1st C)
ST HELEN'S (Northwich)
Pickering W. (11th C)
GHENT
Riley G. (16th C)
ST SEVER
Miller He. (1st C)
PLOEGSTEERT MEM.
Hickson T. (10th C)
ECOIVRES
Ainsworth W.J. (10th C)
BOULOGNE
Gleave J. (10th C)
BRONFAY FARM
Deakin J.W. (10th C)
KEMMEL
Postles H. (1/5th C)
THE HUTS
Clarke E. (10th C)
GEZAINCOURT
Hulme J. (10th C)
BERKS
Kettle A. (10th C)
TAMCAREZ
Southern W. (10th C)
KARASOULI
Connolly J.W.
DOIRAN
Connolly T.H. (12th C)
HODGE CRATER
Baddeley H.S. (18th KL)
REGINA TRENCH
Hunt R. (RE)

HAIDAR PASHA
Webster E. (12th C)
VIS-EN-ARTOIS
Goodier P.L. (DofW)
TOURLAVILLE
Furnival A. (12th C)
AUBY
Miller Ha. (1st C)
HELES MEM.
Bramhall J. (6th S.L)
Tomlinson J. (DofW)
GORRE
Pickering H.E. (1/5thS.L)
PERNES
Connolly L. (1/4thS.L)
YORK (HASPRES)
Jones C.W. (L.F)
GODEWAERSVELDE
Forster S. (A.S.C)
VAUXBUIN
Foxley V.A. (R.F.A)
LAVENTIE
Southern T. (2nd R.B)
POTIJSE
Warburton G.H. (3rd R.B)
LIMERICK
Snelson T. (R.W.F)
OUTTERSTEENE
Smith J. (Welsh)
FERTE-SOUS-JOUARRE-MEM.
Whittaker S. (1st C)
ST JOHN'S L.G.
Garner J. (3rd C)
Hall T. (N.F.)
Marlow G. (L.F.)
Wrench T. (14th C)

Men Who Were First Sons

1st Cheshires
Deakin S.
Deakin W.H.
Whittaker S.
Miller He.

1/5th Cheshires
Deakin J.W.
Postles H.

2nd Cheshires
Sherlock W.

3rd Cheshires
Garner J.

8th Cheshires
Carter C.

10th Cheshires
Adamson J.
Ainsworth W.J.
Buckley J.W.
Clarke E.
Gleave J.H.
Hesketh W.
Hickson T.
Hulme J.
Jones W.
Kelly J.G.
Southern W.
Timmis F.

11th Cheshires
Gregory C.

12th Cheshires
Connolly J.W.
Connolly T.H.
Furnival A.
Webster E.

14th Cheshires
Wrench T.W.

16th Cheshires
Riley G.

2/9th Manchester
Faulkner J.T.

17th Manchester
Snelson G.

18th Kings Liverpool
Baddeley H.S.

1/4th South Lancs.
Connolly L.

Lancs. Fusiliers
Jones C.W.
Marlow G.

Northumberland Fusils
Hall T.

2/6th Royal Warwicks
Johnson H.

Army Service Corps.
Forster S.

2nd Rifle Brigade
Southern T.

3rd Rifle Brigade
Warburton G.H.

77th Norfolks
Miller Ha.

Welsh Regiment
Smith J.

2nd South Wales Borderers
Walsh R.

Canadian Infantry
Davenport T.
Drinkwater W.
Johnson W.

Moving On

THE Lostock Gralam fete of summer 1919 helped the community at large to cast off the all-embracing greatcoat of war and to step into the sunshine of anticipation.

Pre-war, the festivities had been enjoyed by people from across Cheshire and beyond. Large crowds were wont to descend upon the village and extra activities had been designed to exercise both their artistic and physical tastes The fete of 1919 was magnificent both in the events on offer and the attendance it attracted. Furthermore, the glorious sunshine enhanced the splendour of the concourse of local Rose Queens and their retinues. Young men who, a mere twelve months before, had fought at the point of a bayonet in France, were now trying to 'ring' a skittle in the hope of winning a rather sad little goldfish; yellow-skinned women, who had left the Lostock Munitions factory in late 1918, were now in hand-to-hand combat in the egg and spoon race; one or two lads, who had charged, with little more than hope, across the mud of no-man's-land outside Ypres, now pushed their boneshaker bicycles around the coarse grass track on the field next to their old school in pursuit of ½ gallon of rough cider.

Sadly, to the onlookers some 90 years later, the newspaper report of the events on that day read like a roll call of the names of men who had died in the trenches, as their family members strove to put the horrors of 1914-1918 behind them. On Saturday, January 24th 1920 the final act in the village drama was played. For two years a fund-raising committee had been regularly meeting to ensure that a lasting tribute to the boys of Lostock and its adjoining villages could be built. Now after achieving the magnificent sum of £250.00 along with an extra 10 shillings per each inscription, a fifteen feet high Runic cross of Aberdeen marble stood by the road in St. John's churchyard bearing the names of the 65 men who had never returned. In a packed church the Bishop of Chester led the service of commemoration, before the Union Jack was withdrawn from the monument by Mrs Buckley, the landlady of the Black Greyhound public house, who had been unanimously chosen by the whole community in recognition of her tremendous support for the boys with the very regular food parcels sent to the Front and the gifts to wounded soldiers on home recuperation.

One of the many hundreds of street parties to celebrate the Peace.

Brunner Mond's Lostock War Memorial in the 1920s.

Lostock Green

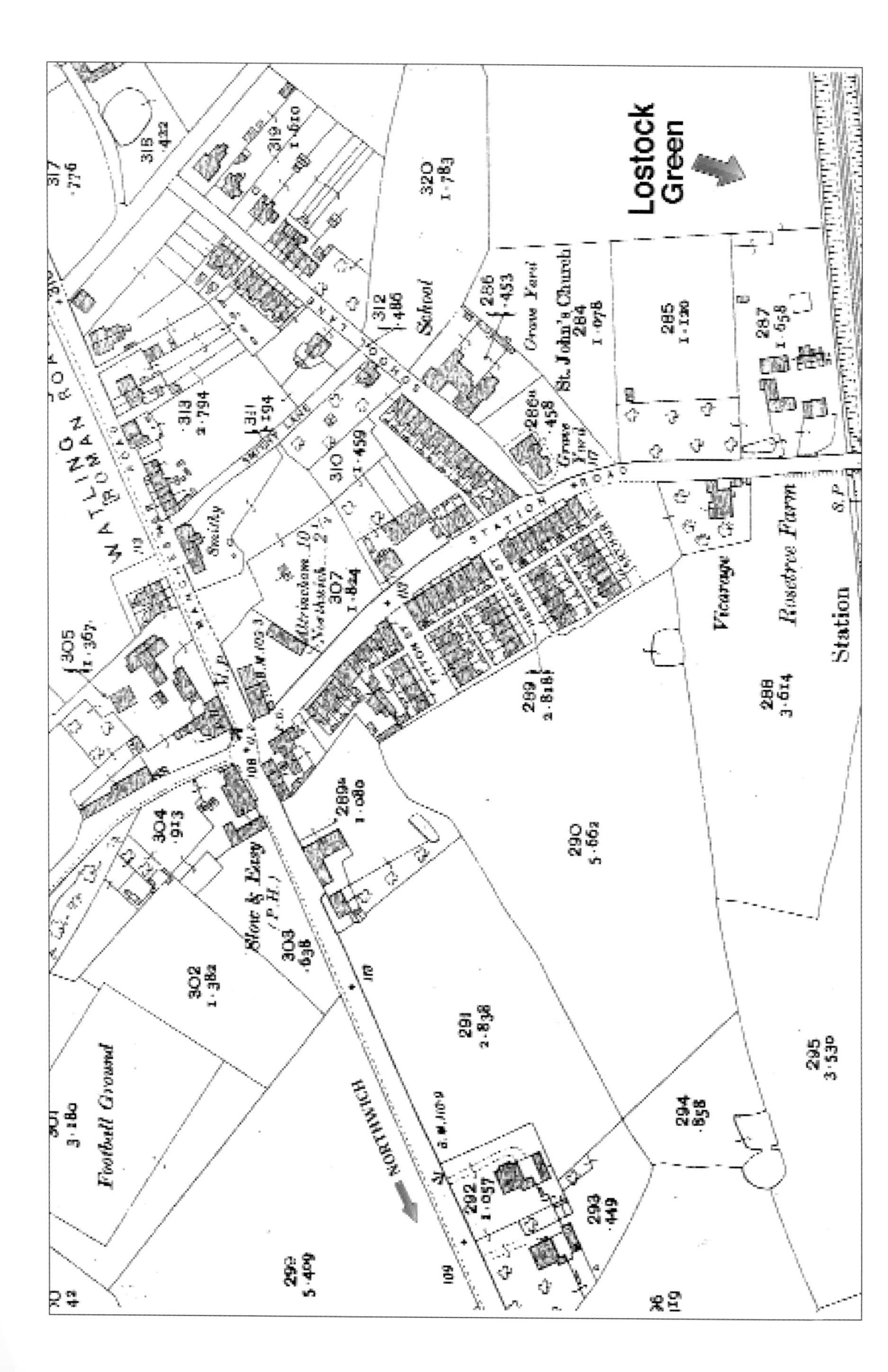

Plot	Area
284	1.078 (St. John's Church)
285	1.190
286	.453
286a	.458 (Grove Farm)
287	1.658
288	3.614 (Rosetree Farm)
289	2.818
289a	1.080
290	5.662
291	2.838
292	1.057
293	.449
294	.858
295	3.530
299	5.409
301	3.180 (Football Ground)
302	1.382
303	.638 (Rose & Crown P.H.)
304	.913
305	1.367
307	1.834 (Wesleyan Methodist Chapel)
310	1.459
311	.194
312	.486 (School)
313	1.794
315	.422
317	.776
319	1.610
320	1.783

Watling Road
Station Road
Northwich
Station
Vicarage
Smithy

Map of Lostock Gralam 1910

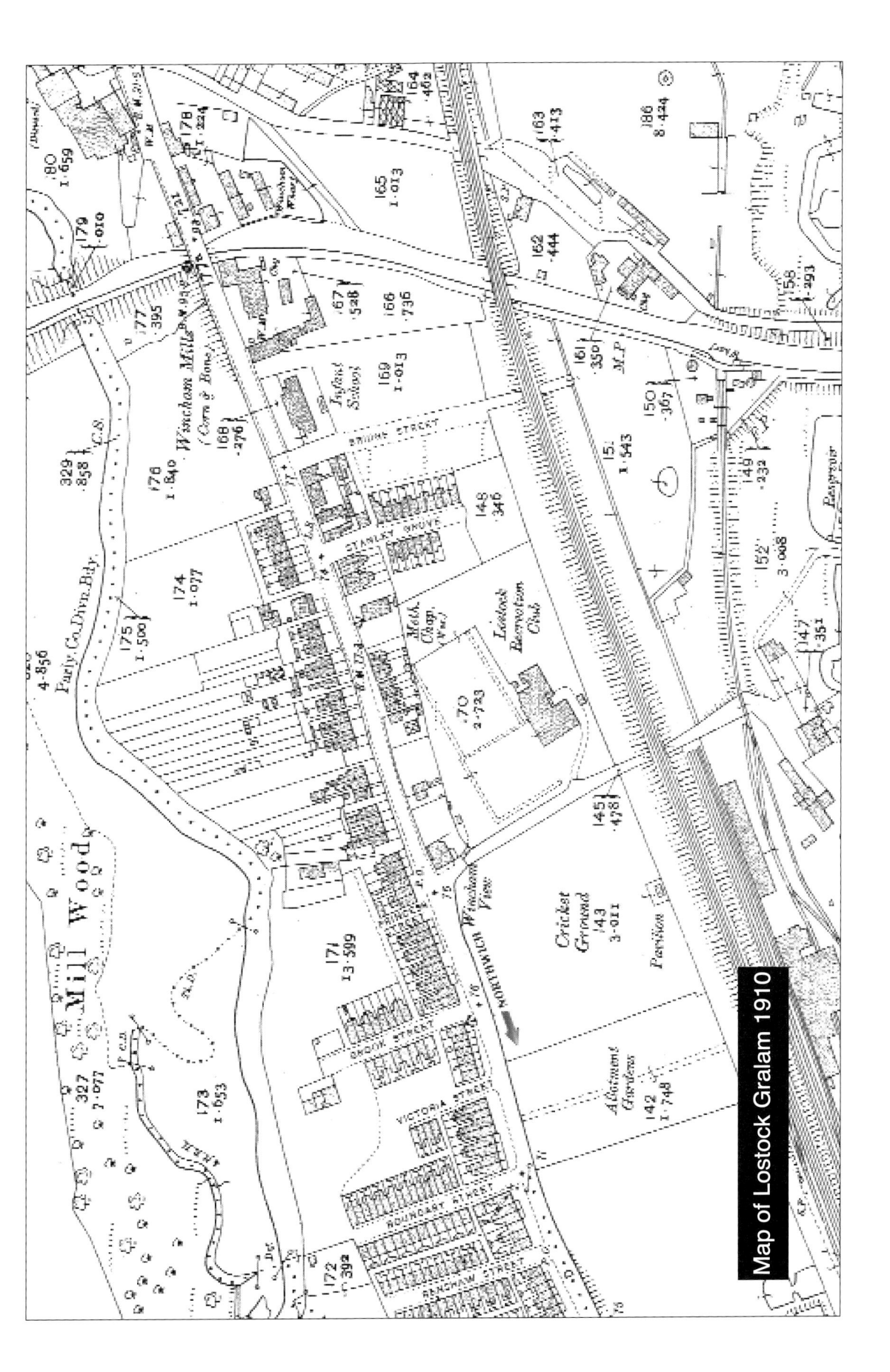

A Peace Arch in Northwich expresses the gratitude of the district and the nation: "Thanks To Our Boys".
(John Chesworth Collection)